CHRIST
—VERSUS—
CAESAR

TWO MASTERS, ONE CHOICE

What others are saying about *Christ versus Caesar*

Should the gospel inform our political views? *Christ versus Caesar* argues in the affirmative—and Connor Boyack makes a persuasive case that following Jesus's teachings means our actions (and therefore the government's) should be based on persuasion and voluntary actions, not mandates and prohibitions.

—Mark Skousen, Presidential Fellow, Chapman University

Intended to resonate not only with Latter-day Saints but also with Christians of any denomination, this book is a beautifully-written, scripturally-grounded, rigorous, and compelling case for why following Christ (and therefore the Golden Rule and the Sermon on the Mount) requires rejecting Caesar (and therefore the state). In short, *Christ versus Caesar* is an eloquent case for why following Jesus has profound political implications we must confront in order to be true disciples.

—Alexandre Christoyannopoulos
Author of *Christian Anarchism: A Political Commentary on the Gospel*

What should Christians "render unto Caesar?" *Christ versus Caesar* is a scripturally sourced response to that important question, which warns Christians they are being "seduced by [Caesar's] statist systems that allow individuals to exert control over their neighbors and be enriched at their expense." This book is important reading for those who wish to avoid that trap and the devastation that inevitably follows.

—Mark Benson Madsen, former state senator

CHRIST
— VERSUS —
CAESAR

TWO MASTERS, ONE CHOICE

CONNOR BOYACK

CFI
An imprint of Cedar Fort, Inc.
Springville, Utah

ISBN 13: 978-1-4621-3888-3

Published by CFI, an imprint of Cedar Fort, Inc.
2373 W. 700 S., Springville, UT 84663
Distributed by Cedar Fort, Inc., www.cedarfort.com

LIBRARY OF CONGRESS CONTROL NUMBER: 2020946376

Cover design by Wes Wheeler
Cover design © 2020 Cedar Fort, Inc.
Edited and Typeset by Heidi Doxey Ford

Printed in the United States of America

10 9 8 7 6 5 4 3 2 1

Printed on acid-free paper

To the humble followers of Christ
who, like me, are trying to figure out
what Jesus meant, and what
it means for us.

CONTENTS

FOREWORD

I am one of those Christians my friend Connor Boyack had in mind when he wrote herein, "A Christian of any particular denomination will find value in this book" and, moreover, that the book is "not meant to convert anyone to my particular views of Christianity."

Connor is a Latter-day Saint, whereas I am a Presbyterian. He did not convert me, but then, he made it plain that conversion wasn't his intention. Without a doubt, I can assert that he was right to predict that I would find value in what he has written. All of these adjectives explain why: informative, passionate, intriguing, challenging, principled, provocative.

Here and there I found passages I plainly disagreed with, though they still made me think. Occasionally, those same passages also pricked my conscience. All too often these days, people read only (or largely) what reinforces the views they already hold. But it doesn't bother me to read things I didn't know or that I might take issue with; I was always taught that a well-rounded and truly educated person knows at least something about views that are new or different.

Of the many verses in scripture that Connor cites, perhaps this one from Psalm 146 best encapsulates his core message:

> Do not put your trust in princes,
> in human beings, who cannot save.
> When their spirit departs, they return to the ground;
> on that very day their plans come to nothing.

Amen to that! Whether you endorse more government, less government, or none at all, you can't honestly survey the lessons of history and conclude that government gets better as it gets bigger. Power is so thoroughly corrupting that I wouldn't trust my best friend with it, let alone someone who fancies himself a prince or a central planner. People who value liberty must always keep an eye on even the best and most humble of their public "servants," which reminds me of something the comedian Groucho Marx once said of his brother Harpo: "He's honest, but you gotta watch him."

In this book, Connor reminds us of the many lies and injustices perpetrated by governments that simultaneously proclaimed their commitment to truth and justice.

In fact, there are so many official lies and injustices in history that an alert and thoughtful citizen should not ignore the fundamental questions Connor raises: Is government a cynical racket or a legitimate representative of "the people"? Might it even be a devilish diversion that undermines faith in the very Highest of authorities? When its actions conflict with good sense or, more importantly, with the teachings of Christ, should a Christian pledge blind allegiance to it anyway?

Government is, by very definition, the only entity in society that can initiate force, legally and routinely. Within broad limits and for self-defense, you and I can use force in retaliation, but we cannot legally strike the first blow. That's a powerful privilege that government reserves to itself—in the form of taxation, conscription, eminent domain, and numerous mandates. As Connor points out, it "can command people to kill others, take their property, control their actions, and coerce them in all manner of ways" and often "without apparent consequence."

Christ warned that we cannot serve two masters, particularly when one contradicts the other. He was referring to money and God, but what about government and God? If one must choose between the two, is there any doubt which one Christ would want you to pick? Connor wants you to think deeply about that, perhaps for the very first time.

Civil disobedience comes in for close attention in this book. If asked, many people would likely say that civil disobedience is never justified, that we should always be patient and work through political channels to get redress for our grievances or to get bad policies changed. That sounds peaceful and appealing on the surface, but I wonder if anybody really believes that. I like what Henry David Thoreau had to say about it: "Must the citizen ever for a moment, or in the least degree, resign his conscience to the legislator? Why has every man a conscience then? I think that we should be men first, and subjects afterward."

It would certainly take a serious flight from conscience for a person to do the "lawful" thing and turn in an escaped slave in 1855. Or to incarcerate an innocent person just because of his race, as Franklin Roosevelt did when he ordered the internment of more than 100,000 Japanese-Americans in 1942. Or to stand idly by in the spring of 2020 as governors ordered virus-infected patients into nursing homes, killing thousands of elderly residents.

Though the one true and flawless King—Jesus Christ—did no wrong, earthly kings do wrong all the time. So do presidents, parliaments, congresses, and your local zoning board. Connor Boyack wants you to rethink the implications of that, for your faith and for the priorities in your life.

I commend Connor, a brother in Christ and a lover of human liberty, for this latest offering. On some critically important matters, it will prompt many readers to get off the fence and take a stand. And in a mixed-up world lacking in solid convictions, that's a good thing.

—Lawrence W. Reed
President Emeritus, Foundation for Economic Education
Author, *Was Jesus a Socialist?*

PROLOGUE

This book is not meant to convert anyone to my particular views on Christianity. This book is also not meant to condemn those whose actions may appear inconsistent with Christ's commandments. As much as anyone else, I am an imperfect person who aims to be considered a saint, but who nevertheless falls short. We are all tempted by the worldly ways of Caesar.

Roughly one-third of people currently living consider themselves Christian.[1] With adherents of Jesus Christ separated into tens of thousands of differing denominations,[2] the reader deserves to know at the outset where this author stands regarding some core claims of Christianity, as this perspective colors the commentary throughout this book. While those of other Christian beliefs—or none—will no doubt find value in this analysis, it is primarily intended for those who share or are not alienated by the author's views.

1. At the time of this writing, the global population is 7.7 billion; see "U.S. and World Population Clock," United States Census Bureau, accessed December 20, 2019, https://www.census.gov/popclock/. An estimated 2.3 billion people are Christian, though the number is likely a conservative estimate, since it relies upon official church membership figures, and many others might consider themselves Christian who have not affiliated with a church; see "Christians are the largest religious group in 2015," Pew Research Center, accessed December 20, 2019, https://www.pewforum.org/2017/04/05/the-changing-global-religious-landscape/pf_17-04-05_projectionsupdate_grl310px/.
2. Scott Eric Alt, "We Need to Stop Saying That There Are 33,000 Protestant Denominations," *National Catholic Register*, February 9, 2016, https://www.ncregister.com/blog/scottericalt/we-need-to-stop-saying-that-there-are-33000-protestant-denominations.

I believe in Jesus Christ. I believe that we are children of a Heavenly Father. And I believe that God the Father loves His children regardless of where or to whom they were born. I believe He wants all of us to return to His presence. And so, I believe that He has communicated through prophets to teach us what is required.[3]

I not only believe in Jesus Christ, I believe Jesus Christ. I take His words at face value when He told His disciples in Jerusalem, "Other sheep I have, which are not of this fold: them also I must bring, and they shall hear my voice; and there shall be one fold, and one shepherd."[4] Accordingly, I do not believe in a closed canon; I believe that Christ has spoken to others, as He said.

This claim causes angst for many Christians, as they were raised to believe that the Bible is the beginning and end of God's word. In defense of this position, they often point to the book of Revelation, where we read, "For I testify unto every man that heareth the words of . . . this book, If any man shall add unto these things, God shall add unto him the plagues that are written in this book."[5] But biblical scholars widely understand what those who employ this argument apparently do not: this verse applies only to the book of Revelation. Many other New Testament "books" were written after John received his revelation on the Isle of Patmos, and, more to the point, the Bible as we know it did not exist at the time. For centuries following John's revelation, manuscripts were circulated throughout the early Christian community individually or in combination. Of the entire corpus of 5,366 known Greek New Testament manuscripts, only 35 contain the whole New Testament as we now know it, and 34 of those were compiled after A.D. 1000.

So, yes, I believe in additional revelation beyond what was eventually included in the Bible. I believe that God has spoken in modern times as well as in ancient, and that He has provided additional revelations to help His children better know how to return to His presence. I welcome these additional teachings, especially because they provide clarity and context for teachings from the Bible. This book will therefore avail itself of all these teachings in order to better understand the contrast between Christ and Caesar.[6] And while these additional scriptures will be cited for support, this

3. Amos 3:7.
4. John 10:16.
5. Revelation 22:18.
6. This is especially important since various biblical passages have been cited both by political rulers to demand obedience and by their subjects to justify resistance and liberation. Additional clarity to resolve the conflict should be welcomed.

book's arguments will be helpful and appealing to all who share a belief in Christ's New Testament teachings.

If it is not already apparent to the reader, allow me to be more succinct: I am a member of The Church of Jesus Christ of Latter-day Saints. But before you close the book, let me caution you: the observations and criticisms contained within apply as much to my faith community as to any other. A Christian of any particular denomination will find value in this book.

A final word about my perspective in writing this book. Mortal rulers come in many forms: Caesar, Pharaoh, or Führer; king, emperor, or president. Each form of government has different aspects and degrees of evil, yet they share common characteristics that help us paint a picture to understand how Christ's counsel might apply today. For simplicity and to symbolically continue the references found in the gospels, the use of "Caesar" in this book is therefore used as an abstract reference to earthly rulers and governments generally. It also involves and implies the puppeteers pulling the strings behind the scene: Satan and his forces who build up their kingdom using idols, false prophets, and counterfeits to God, our only legitimate Ruler. Caesar, as referenced in this book, is the institutionalized antithesis to Jesus.

Christ's teachings serve as a reference point for our behavior. We may stray from the path, but He shows us how to return. Unfortunately, many followers have blinded themselves to some of the plain teachings of Jesus Christ pertaining to political matters. Our task is to open our eyes and return to the strait and narrow path. Let's proceed together.

INTRODUCTION

The sun shone brightly on rural Litchfield, Illinois, one morning in 1940 as a caravan of twenty-one automobiles with nearly one hundred Jehovah's Witnesses descended on the city to distribute literature and seek converts. The city's population barely exceeded 7,000,[1] and some of the locals tried to chase them out of town. For nearly two miles, rowdy residents from Litchfield chased the Witnesses on poorly maintained roads until they blocked the highway, forcing them to stop. The men and women were pulled out of their cars, and the men were beaten for several minutes.[2] This was not simple religious bigotry; it was a direct response to the Witnesses' political views and allegedly insufficient patriotism.

While others in the mob devoted themselves to destroying the Witnesses' literature and personal property—twelve of their vehicles were destroyed beyond repair—others threw the Witnesses to the ground and repeatedly kicked them. Some of the men were dragged over to a nearby car, where an American flag had been spread out. The city's chief of police sat in a nearby car, silently watching the spectacle unfold as the mob repeatedly bashed a man's head against the flag-adorned vehicle[3]—his punishment for being unwilling to salute the flag.

---

1. The 1940 census showed 7,048 residents in Litchfield, Illinois. See "Population of Incorporated Places: 1940 and 1930," United States Census Bureau, accessed December 20, 2019, https://www2.census.gov/library/publications/decennial/1940/population-volume-1/33973538v1ch04.pdf.
2. "The Persecution of Jehovah's Witnesses," American Civil Liberties Union, January 1941, http://debs.indstate.edu/a505p4_1941.pdf.
3. Ibid.

In all, 64 of the Witnesses were beaten that day in an attempt to force them to display proper deference to the flag. This horrifying scenario was not an aberration that year. An estimated 1,500 Witnesses were assaulted in 335 separate attacks.[4] In an outburst of violence "unparalleled in America since the attack on the Mormons"[5] a century earlier, supposedly patriotic Americans suddenly and violently attacked fellow citizens who were deemed insufficiently loyal to the government.

These were not solely the acts of isolated ruffians, either. Prominent voices called for the expulsion of the Witnesses and other individuals like them. One newspaper editorial in Jackson, Mississippi, captured the sentiment shared by others:

> Departure under pressure of a colony of "Jehovah's Witnesses" camped on the Pocahontas Road just beyond the city limits was proper disposal of what threatened to become a serious situation. There is no room in Jackson or vicinity for any person who will not salute the American flag and openly says he will not fight for his country under any circumstances. It so happens that sturdy citizens of Jackson don't believe in nonsense of that sort and will not tolerate its existence in or near this community.

And to think, these attacks all started with a third-grader. In September 1935, young Carleton Nicholls stood for, but refused to recite, the Pledge of Allegiance. The Nicholls family were Jehovah's Witnesses, and—just months prior—their church's president, Joseph Rutherford, had argued that reciting the pledge was tantamount to worshiping a graven image, something prohibited by the Bible. Rutherford said that the "nations of the world are under the control of Satan the Devil" and that requiring a "child of God to salute the national flag compels that person to salute the Devil as the invisible god of the nation."[6] For Witnesses, the flag became an idol to avoid.

Eight-year-old Carleton was targeted by his teacher for being unwilling to pledge allegiance to the flag. Supported by his father, who joined him in class, young Carleton remained seated while the students were told to rise and salute the flag. "I will stand for no such insult to the American flag!" the principal raged. After refusing to leave, Mr. Nicholls and an associate who had joined him were taken to jail.[7] Rutherford shone a spotlight

---

4. Ibid.
5. Ibid.
6. Steven K. Green, *The Third Disestablishment: Church, State, and American Culture, 1940–1975* (New York: Oxford University Press, 2019), 67.
7. Susan Dudley Gold, *Saluting the Flag: West Virginia State Board of Education v. Barnette* (New York: Cavendish Square Publishing, 2014), 28–29.

on the incident, fueling media coverage, which inspired other Witnesses to follow Carleton's example. Within a year, more than 120 children had been expelled from schools for refusing to salute the flag—a behavior that the adherents had made part of their doctrine.[8]

Rutherford was determined to press the issue in pursuit of religious freedom. He made it clear that refusing to salute the flag did not convey a "disrespect of the flag or for the country but . . . a proper respect and obedience to almighty God." Their actions were intended not to cause pointless confrontation, but to practice their faith. Jehovah's Witnesses, he said, would "not violate any of the laws of the state that are in harmony with God's law. But if a law of the state is in direct violation of God's law, they will obey God's law first and all the time."[9]

Carleton's family sued the state, seeking a return to school. They argued in their petition that compulsory pledges of allegiance violated the boy's freedom of religion. On appeal, the Massachusetts Supreme Judicial Court dealt a blow to Witnesses by dismissing the claim. The justices opined:

> There is nothing in the salute or the pledge of allegiance which constitutes an act of idolatry, or which approaches to any religious observance. It does not in any reasonable sense hurt, molest, or restrain a human being in respect to "worshipping God" within the meaning of words in the Constitution. The rule and the statute are well within the competency of legislative authority. They exact nothing in opposition to religion. They are directed to a justifiable end in the conduct of education in the public schools.[10]

The black-robed lawyers on the Court further argued that the pledge was proper in order to instill in students "patriotism and . . . a recognition of the blessing conferred by orderly government."[11] Courts elsewhere concurred. The New Jersey Supreme Court, for example, said in 1937 that the pledge "is, by no stretch of the imagination, a religious rite," but rather a "patriotic ceremony."[12] A year later, California's Supreme Court claimed that the flag salute was one of the "social and patriotic duties of the citizens" required to maintain "good order, safety and the public welfare of the nation."[13] Making youth pledge allegiance to the flag "tend[s] to stimulate" in their minds "sentiments of lasting affection and respect for and unflattering loyalty to our

---

8. Green, *The Third Disestablishment*, 67.
9. Gold, *Saluting the Flag*, 31.
10. *Carleton B. Nicholls, Jr., vs. Mayor and School Committee of Lynn*, 297 Mass. 65.
11. Ibid.
12. *Hering v. State Board of Education*, 189 A. 629 (N.J. 1937).
13. *Gabrielli v. Knickerbocker*, 12 Cal.2d 85.

government and its institutions," they said.[14] In turn, some states passed criminal statutes that added teeth to school district policies, including prison time and fines for influencing children not to salute the flag—effectively criminalizing religious belief and punishing parental teaching.[15]

As controversial as these cases were, the physical persecution against Witnesses came because of a case sparked in Pennsylvania by Walter Gobitas and his two children. Walter had been inspired by Carleton and others like him, and instructed his two children, Lillian and Billy, not to pledge allegiance to the flag at school. Billy's teacher was so upset about his failure to pledge that she tried to force his arm into the air to make the salute.[16] Lillian's teacher had a different response, hugging the young student and praising her for her valor,[17] despite being bullied by other children who threw stones at her while yelling things like, "Here comes Jehovah!"[18] The response of Lillian's teacher can likely be explained, in part, by the fact that she was a Quaker, a faith tradition that had experienced its own persecution in the past.[19]

For their part, school officials unsurprisingly refused to budge, and the children were promptly expelled. Backed by legal support from their church and the ACLU, the Gobitas family's case was randomly assigned to Judge Albert Branson Maris, who was also a Quaker. His 1938 decision was rather blunt:

> The flag salute by children who are sincerely opposed to it upon conscientious religious grounds is not a reasonable method of teaching

---

14. Ibid.
15. Green, *The Third Disestablishment*, 67–68.
16. At the time, Americans pledged allegiance with what is now known as the "Hitler salute"—arm fully extended toward the flag, palm down. As the Nazis gained power and the action was associated with their oppressive regime, tension arose in America due to the similarity. Organizations such as the Parent and Teachers Association, Boy Scouts of America, and the Red Cross, agitated for a change. Congress later modified the federal Flag Code in 1942, instructing Americans to place their hand over their heart instead.
17. Jeffrey Owen Jones and Peter Meyer, *The Pledge: A History of the Pledge of Allegiance* (New York: Thomas Dunne Books, 2010), 122.
18. "Lilian Gobitas Interview on Experiences with Persecution," Robert H. Jackson Center, accessed December 20, 2019, https://www.youtube.com/watch?v=eGjfsUw5Dw4.
19. Pennsylvania was a good place to pursue the legal battle, given the prevalence of Quakers in the area. The state was founded by William Penn, a Quaker himself, who had been arrested and charged with illegal preaching in England for trying to openly share his beliefs. Penn intentionally provoked a legal battle in which he was later successful. He set up his new American colony to be a safe haven for practitioners of alternative religions looking to escape the crushing intolerance of the Crown—Quakers, Huguenots, Mennonites, Amish, Lutherans, and more.

> civics . . . but tends to have the contrary effect upon such children. Our country's safety surely does not depend upon the totalitarian idea of forcing all citizens into one common mold of thinking and acting or requiring them to render a lip service of loyalty in a manner which conflicts with their sincere religious convictions.[20]

Maris asserted that officials were not "empowered to censor another's religious convictions or set boundaries to the areas of human conduct in which those convictions control his actions, unless compelled to do so by an overwhelming public necessity."[21] A judge had finally recognized, in America, that forced patriotism could violate religious belief, after Witnesses were repeatedly told by other judges how their religious beliefs were not in any way negatively impacted by the compulsory loyalty. It was a temporary victory, however. On appeal, the US Supreme Court overturned lower courts on the 1940 Gobitas case and upheld the right of schools to expel non-conforming children in an 8-1 opinion. Chief Justice Hughes asserted that "the state can insist on inculcation of loyalty."[22]

This Supreme Court ruling—and its public implication that Witnesses were disloyal—was all certain American "patriots" needed to oppress their nonpledging neighbors who refused to outwardly exhibit loyalty to America and its flag. The attacks began in earnest. One sheriff, when asked by a reporter why Witnesses were being run out of town, responded, "They're traitors; the Supreme Court says so. Ain't you heard?"[23]

To some extent, this horrible reaction is predictable. "Think not that I am come to send peace on earth," Jesus taught his disciples. "I came not to send peace, but a sword."[24] Those who follow Christ must embrace the implications of His message, and that means parting ways, in some circumstances, with those who reject it. While God wants all to become disciples, it is inevitable that not all will choose to follow Him; Christ's message therefore causes division. We must choose. God does not want "lukewarm"[25] people who cannot pick a side. The Jehovah's Witnesses had chosen their side and were acting in accordance with that decision. Loyalty to Christ means, for them, not professing loyalty to any competing authorities.

---

20. Jones, *The Pledge*, 123.
21. Green, *The Third Disestablishment*, 68.
22. Ibid., 69.
23. Shawn Francis Peters, *Judging Jehovah's Witnesses: Religious Persecution and the Dawn of Rights Revolution* (Lawrence, Kansas: University Press of Kansas, 2000), 84.
24. Matthew 10:34.
25. Revelation 3:16.

Those who believe in Jesus Christ—and *believe* Him—recognize His right to rule; He is king. Our loyalty is to God. We are all God's children; we are one family. Thus, true disciples of Christ do not listen to other authorities that tell them to hold animosity toward or indifference about other people merely because they speak a different language, come from a different culture, or practice a different religion. We should not be tribal creatures that let imaginary lines on a map—the result of unjust wars and political conquests—define our loyalties and affections.

We recognize in the persecution of the Jehovah's Witnesses a sincerity that is often not exhibited by most Christians, including, potentially, ourselves—indeed, most self-professed followers of Christ are content to embrace two masters. Whether through apathetic indifference or awkward compartmentalization that requires ignoring clear scriptures to the contrary, these individuals attend their local chapel for worship services but frequent their summer cottage in Babylon.[26] And yet Christ is clear: no man can serve two masters.[27] We must choose whom we will serve.[28] Chief Justice Hughes rightly pointed out that the state demands loyalty, and Caesar impresses it upon the rising generation. Such propaganda is the hallmark of every state and always justified by its functionaries.

While the Jehovah's Witnesses standing up for their faith are a recent example, similar examples are by no means unique or uncommon. Indeed, God's people have often, when practicing their faith fully, found themselves in conflict with secular authority and the culture that supports it. Christians are generally familiar with the persecution heaped upon the early saints by Rome, but some wrongly believe that this persecution was because of Christians' worship of Jesus. Rather, the persecution was a result of their unwillingness to worship the Roman emperor. Rome tolerated many religions, but demanded loyalty to the state above them all; numerous feasts and festivals were designed to create imperial unity and cultivate loyalty, but when Christians refused to participate, they were seen as disloyal. Since they refused to offer sacrifices or light incense to the gods, Christians were seen as subversive to the social order and, therefore, were harassed and executed by secular authorities.

While Caesar demands our loyalty, so too does God. What, then, is a disciple of Christ to do? How do we resolve these competing claims, if we can at all? Scripture is filled with examples where this conflict plays

26. Neal A. Maxwell, *A Wonderful Flood of Light* (Salt Lake City: Bookcraft, 1990), 47.
27. Matthew 6:24.
28. Joshua 24:15.

out—often, unfortunately, resulting in the saints siding with the secular state. What does all this mean for those of us living in modern times? Can we be patriotic and still follow God's commandments to abstain from idolatry? Can we support the state but also maintain our submission to God? Can we be "good citizens" and also dedicated followers of Christ? In short, what would it look like if we took the Savior at His word and closely followed His commandment to serve and follow only Him? These are the questions we will explore in this book—questions that have significant implications for all who try, albeit imperfectly, to have "an eye single to the glory of God."[29]

Overt persecution did not succeed in weakening the resolve of early Christians; martyrdom actually facilitated evangelism and encouraged the gospel's dissemination by others seeking resurrection and salvation. And so, when Constantine came around, the strategy shifted: church and state were intertwined, and Christianity was "officially adopted" by Caesar. The centuries since have invoked theological chaos and confusion, enabled by scholars and priests who along the way have articulated all sorts of defenses in support of Caesar, contrary to the actions and beliefs of the early disciples, who took Christ's message for what it implied, which includes renouncing any loyalty to Caesar. Indeed, the greatest threat to Christianity has not been from external threats but from internal dissension and dilution of doctrine.

It is the thesis of this book that many Christians today have failed to separate Christ from Caesar, often because they fail to recognize the modern implications of scriptural warnings about Babylon, Caesar, and the secular state. Christians let their loyalties waffle between the two, lavishing both with their affections. Effectively they try to serve two masters at once, contrary to Christ's clear statement on the matter. This book presents a simple question with an obvious answer that is apparently difficult for many Christians to comply with: *to which master should men be loyal*? The task before us is to peel back the centuries of corrosive conflation between Christ and Caesar and explore what a disciple of the former ought to do in rejecting the latter. This task is not for the faint of heart. But then again, none of Christ's doctrine is.

---

29. Doctrine and Covenants 4:5.

CHRIST AND CAESAR IN CONTEXT

Vincenzo Guo Xijin is a Christian in China—an affiliation that comes, as you might imagine, with many problems. These problems are exacerbated for Guo because he is in a position of leadership within the Catholic church. Since the Communist state was founded in 1949, there has been tension between the Vatican and Chinese leadership. Officially atheist, the Communist Party nevertheless allows for "normal religious activity," which is limited to activities taking place within government-sanctioned religious organizations and registered places of worship.[1]

For Catholics, the state-approved church is called the Chinese Patriotic Catholic Association, and it is governed not by the Pope, but by Communist leadership. The state selects ministers, censors religious material,[2] and keeps a close eye to ensure that outside influences—in this case, the Vatican—do not threaten Party control. As a result, an underground church emerged, one that is faithful to the Vatican but not recognized by Chinese authorities.

Bishop Guo was asked by the Vatican to step aside and allow another individual to be the bishop instead—Vincent Zhan Silu, who was excommunicated in 2011 after being installed as bishop by the Communists in

1. "Freedom of Religion in China," Wikipedia, accessed December 27, 2019, https://en.wikipedia.org/wiki/Freedom_of_religion_in_China.
2. "China Bans Online Bible Sales as It Tightens Religious Controls," *The Boston Globe*, April 5, 2018, https://www.bostonglobe.com/news/world/2018/04/05/china-bans-online-bible-sales-tightens-religious-controls/t2y731JyPR43POc-n03pbbM/story.html.

2000 without Vatican approval.[3] Guo obliged, but was still unwilling to align himself with the Communist-controlled church, nor would he encourage his priests and congregants to do so. Party bosses followed, monitored, and visited Guo for months, attempting to pressure him into signing an agreement to affiliate with the state-controlled church. A Vatican-affiliated news agency explained: "Authorities have been exerting pressure, blackmailing and threatening priests to push them to sign this accession in exchange for government recognition without which their ministry is forbidden."[4] In a letter to the government, Guo wrote:

> The government has already decided to persecute priests who refuse to sign the request [for membership in the Chinese Patriotic Catholic Association]. If I am unable to protect them, it is not worth my time to be recognized as an auxiliary bishop. I am willing to face persecution together with other priests.[5]

The former cardinal of Hong Kong has openly criticized the concessions made by the Vatican in hopes of gaining recognition by and access to China. Cardinal Joseph Zen flew to the Vatican to air his concerns directly with the Pope and later went public with the confidential agreement the Vatican had made to undo Zhan's excommunication and install him as a bishop, a move approved both by the Vatican and Chinese authorities.[6] Pope Francis told Cardinal Zen that he had told his aides "not to create another Mindszenty case"—a reference to a Hungarian cardinal, Józef Mindszenty, who had vocally opposed both fascism and communism, and who was imprisoned by the Nazis and then tortured by the Communists. Pope Paul VI, under pressure from Hungarian authorities, eventually stripped Mindszenty of his religious authority. During this time, some felt that "the Vatican cared more about offending the Kremlin than defending religious believers. Of course,

---

3. "Is the Mindong Case a "stress test" for Sino-Vatican relations?," La Stampa, March 30, 2018, https://www.lastampa.it/vatican-insider-en/2018/03/30/news/is-the-mindong-case-a-stress-test-for-sino-vatican-relations-1.33999218.
4. "China pressuring priest at center of agreement with Vatican," ABC News, November 22, 2019, https://abcnews.go.com/International/wireStory/china-pressuring-priest-center-agreement-vatican-67221304.
5. "Msgr. Guo Xijin: Persecution is preferable to joining the Patriotic Association," AsiaNews.it, June 18, 2019, http://www.asianews.it/news-en/Msgr.-Guo-Xijin:-Persecution-is-preferable-to-joining-the-Patriotic-Association-47315.html.
6. "Vatican courts China with plan to install excommunicated bishop," *The Guardian*, January 30, 2018, https://www.theguardian.com/world/2018/jan/30/vatican-china-ties-excommunicated-bishop-hong-kong-cardinal-shantou.

the opposite was the goal; but the actual effect sometimes looked timid, craven, self-defeating."[7]

Put simply, the goal of Chinese authorities is to control and subdue religious elements that pose a threat to their rule. To that end, they are comfortable only with installing state-friendly ministers whom they can bring to heel when necessary, or whom they never have to bring to heel, because they owe their position to the state, not to the church. And so, many Christians are perplexed why there is an attempt to negotiate with a hostile government that wants to eliminate, not accommodate, their religion. "Why should the Catholic Church participate in its own dissolution and destruction?" one Catholic observer said,[8] echoing concerns shared by other Christian groups in the country who face restrictions on teaching their faith to their children, getting baptized, and preaching what they believe.[9] Chinese Christians face mandates to remove depictions of Jesus and replace them with Communist state leaders; as one pastor reported, "The government is trying to eliminate our belief and wants to become God instead of Jesus."[10]

In contrast, for many Christians around the world, affiliating with their faith is not controversial or demanding; it is easy to claim to worship Jesus. But stories such as this one suggest that remaining faithful during times of persecution and corruption is what really demonstrates someone's commitment to Christ. Do we compromise with Caesar and his competing demands or stubbornly refuse to concede? Can a disciple of Christ support the state? If so, how oppressive must it be before that support should be revoked? And how should a Christian act in regard to governments that are seemingly democratic, protective of religious freedom, and constitutionally limited to supposedly protect individual rights? Should Christians in China resist their government, while their American counterparts co-mingle with the state?

---

7. Paul Kengor, "Pope Francis and the Cardinal Mindszenty Treatment in China," *Crisis Magazine*, February 12, 2018, https://www.crisismagazine.com/2018/pope-francis-cardinal-mindszenty-treatment-china.
8. "Social scientist: Vatican is 'negotiating the surrender' of China's real Church to the Communists," *Life Site News*, February 5, 2018, https://www.lifesitenews.com/news/social-scientist-vatican-is-negotiating-the-surrender-of-chinas-real-church.
9. "China BANS Christian children from attending church and threaten parents with legal action," *Daily Express*, July 30, 2016, https://www.express.co.uk/news/world/694830/China-BANS-children-from-attending-church-and-threaten-parents-with-legal-action.
10. "China tells Christians to renounce faith in Jesus & worship President Xi Jinping instead," *Christian Today*, July 19, 2020, https://www.christiantoday.com/article/china-tells-christians-renounce-faith-in-jesus-worship-president-xi-jinping/135221.htm.

Scriptural history informs us that God's people become more earnest and more faithful with opposition; "for whom the Lord loveth he chasteneth."[11] In modern times, God pointed out that "my people must needs be chastened until they learn obedience, if it must needs be, by the things which they suffer."[12] It is one thing for Christians to remain faithful when persecuted by a hostile Caesar; many scripture stories lead us to praise God's faithful who remained loyal to God above all else.[13] It is another thing entirely when Caesar appears nonthreatening and eager to collaborate. God's commandment to side with Him permits no exceptions when Caesar's demeanor or demands appear soothing and simple. And so, we must be especially on guard when finding ourselves in environments that are *not* like they are in China, or were in Hungary; our commitments to discipleship may face their greatest challenge in times when fellow Christians perceive Caesar as friendly or worthy of support.

For some Christians, the extent of their worship involves going to church a few times a year and thinking about God that often. For others, it is enough to have been "saved," as if it were a single event in one's past, a milestone to move on from and reference as needed or when convenient. But Christ demands more than mere lip service to His teachings. "This people draweth nigh unto me with their mouth," Jesus said, quoting Isaiah, "and honoureth me with their lips; but their heart is far from me." And then, the kicker: "But in vain they do worship me, teaching for doctrines the commandments of men."[14] It is as the apostle Paul told Timothy: people would "turn away their ears from the truth, and shall be turned unto fables."[15] It is convenient to affiliate with Christ while your heart is with Team Caesar; it is another thing to believe Christ and follow Him, especially when the culture considers such behavior to be unpatriotic, fringe, or extreme.

Paul warned Timothy of a time in which people "will not endure sound doctrine, but after their own lusts shall they heap to themselves teachers, having itching ears."[16] It is not that remarkable of a prophecy, perhaps, since it describes an apparent human condition: God's people had long been watering down His doctrine to suit their comfort level, preferring those who preached easy, affirming messages to others who rebuked the people's

11. Hebrews 12:6
12. Doctrine and Covenants 105:6; see also Doctrine and Covenants 1:27.
13. Acts 5:29; Exodus 1:22; 2:2; 7–10; Jeremiah 22:13–19; Matthew 2:13; Daniel 3:4–6, 12; 6:7–10.
14. Matthew 15:8–9.
15. 2 Timothy 4:4.
16. 2 Timothy 4:3.

apostasy.[17] But God "had compassion on his people" and "sent to them . . . messengers" in order to teach the gospel. Yet the tendency to "go along to get along" with society is and always has been strong, so "they mocked the messengers of God, and despised his words, and misused his prophets,"[18] repeating a pattern that unfortunately fills the scriptural record.

Have you ever wondered why God's people constantly fashioned idols to worship? Moses was delayed on Mount Sinai, which led the children of Israel to demand that Aaron "make us gods"[19] to praise and follow. A golden calf was fashioned as the object of worship, showing the ongoing influence of the Egyptian religion and culture among the people. It is evident that "in their hearts they turned back to Egypt,"[20] unable to overcome the spiritual and emotional pull of their previous life. It is a cycle we see repeated in the Bible: monotheistic Jews were constantly surrounded—and conquered—by other people who believed in different or multiple gods. The temptation to blend in with society was evidently overpowering at times. In time, Israel "walked in the statutes of the heathen" and "feared other gods," going so far as to build altars to these gods right in their communities in order to more easily participate in pagan rituals.[21]

It is easy for a modern reader to set these stories aside as irrelevant. Surely we are *nothing* like these wayfaring Israelites with pagan tendencies. We are faithfully monotheistic, for starters; we would not be caught dead worshiping a cow. But where Moses lifted up a brass serpent to physically heal the injured Israelites who would look at it,[22] Jesus later taught that He would be spiritually lifted up to offer eternal life to all who would look unto Him.[23] And where Israel once worshiped physical idols, our idolatry is more spiritual, sophisticated, and modern.

But we are no less tempted by carnal loyalties and power than our wilderness-wandering brothers and sisters from biblical times.

The idolatrous Israelites "rejoiced in the works of their own hands,"[24] and therein lies the central theme of this book's analysis. Idolatry is not merely about stupidly worshiping a man-made object. It is also about honoring and supporting man-made institutions as a replacement for God. It

17. 2 Chronicles 18:7; 36:15–16; Isaiah 30:10; Helaman 13:24–27.
18. 2 Chronicles 36:15–16.
19. Exodus 32:1.
20. Acts 7:39.
21. 2 Kings 17:7–13.
22. Numbers 21:4–9.
23. John 3:14–15.
24. Acts 7:41; see also Psalm 115:4–8.

is about relying upon and deifying the arm of flesh. Do we fear and follow God, or man? Christ wants us to trust and have faith in Him. He had already shown Israel how He could guide and provide for them, and yet they wanted to take matters into their own hands. They turned their backs on the Deliverer out of a desire to secure protection and prosperity for themselves—the whole point of pagan sacrifice.

Our modern idols can be "any thing that is in the heaven above, or that is in the earth beneath." God states that "thou shalt not bow down thyself to them, nor serve them: for I the Lord thy God am a jealous God."[25] But why? Why should God demand our loyalty and makes us choose between Him and, well, basically everything else?

Who Was Jesus?

Jesus Christ is King,[26] and from this simple statement flows all the problems with Caesar.

Known by many names,[27] Jesus's given name was *Yeshua* in Hebrew and means "Jehovah saves." During his life, he would have been called *Yeshua Bar Yehosef* ("Jesus, son of Joseph") or *Yeshua Nasraya* ("Jesus of Nazareth") to identify and separate him from the other Yeshuas around, as it was a common name at the time.[28] As His ministry began, disciples recognized in Jesus the fulfillment of past prophecies about a king who would rule all nations and save Israel. They began calling him their Messiah, the anointed one. ("Christ" comes from the Greek translation of the word.) In the Old Testament, God instructed prophets to anoint a person and proclaim him king, signifying that God had Himself given that person authority to act as His representative.[29] Thus, calling Jesus the Messiah, or Christ, was rich in meaning for those who began using the term—it was a recognition that this

---

25. Exodus 20:4–5.

26. Isaiah goes further, saying that "The Lord is our judge, the Lord is our lawgiver, the Lord is our king" (Isaiah 33:22)—comprising judicial, legislative, and executive functions. He is not just King, but the Alpha and Omega—the beginning and the end—of all authority. See also 2 Nephi 10:14.

27. "Jesus Christ, Names and Titles of," *The Encyclopedia of Mormonism*, accessed December 27, 2019, https://eom.byu.edu/index.php/Jesus_Christ,_Names_and_Titles_of.

28. Brian Palmer, "Happy Birthday, Dear Yeshua, Happy Birthday to You!," *Slate*, December 24, 2008, https://slate.com/news-and-politics/2008/12/was-jesus-a-common-name-back-when-he-was-alive.html.

29. 1 Samuel 15:1, 17; 1 Kings 19:15–16; 2 Kings 9:3; 11:12; 23:30; 2 Samuel 12:7.

man was the foretold king who would save God's people. Jesus Christ was and is the Savior anointed by God to rule His kingdom.

That was, of course, a point of contention for the earthly kings who claimed political authority over the area. Consider Herod, the "client king" whom Rome allowed to rule in Judea after they conquered it in 63 B.C. When the visiting wise men sought a new "King of the Jews,"[30] Herod was "troubled" and unsurprisingly eager to learn the child's location and identity. Already, Herod had killed close members of his own family who posed a threat to his jealous rule.[31] Herod asked the chief priests and scribes about the report, and they told him that a prophecy suggested Bethlehem as the location. Falsely claiming to want to worship the child as well, Herod instructed the wise men to return and reveal the child's identity to him once they learned it. As the story goes, the travelers were warned in a dream not to tell Herod, who then slaughtered all the baby boys in Bethlehem and the surrounding area in order to snuff out his competition.[32] Jesus and his family, of course, had already escaped to Egypt. Thus began the life of God's Anointed One on earth, facing from the outset a political threat from a self-declared rival.

Jesus was born into a world of sociopolitical tension. Many Jews believed themselves to be living in the last days and yearned for the long-promised Messiah to save them from their oppressive rulers and become their new political king. As the disciples of Jesus began applying the label to Him, it was not a simple platitude. There was a very real hope that Christ would be a sort of warrior priest, assembling an army to overthrow both the Herodian dynasty and the Roman occupation. This explains the confusion among His followers when they had to confront the reality that this was not what Christ actually came to do.[33]

Jesus was not a revolutionary in the conventional, insurrectional sense, but his actions and teachings were indeed quite revolutionary. Though He came not to abolish but to fulfill the existing law,[34] Christ's actions (associating with "unclean" people like publicans, lepers, and Samaritans) and teachings (loving

---

30. Matthew 2:2.
31. "Herod, King of Judea," *Encyclopedia Brittanica*, accessed December 27, 2019, https://www.britannica.com/biography/Herod-king-of-Judaea.
32. Contrary to the huge massacre often envisioned, it is likely that given the population at the time, there were only a dozen or two babies killed at most. See "Truth or Fiction: Did Herod Really Slaughter Baby Boys in Bethlehem?," Desiring God, December 22, 2015, https://www.desiringgod.org/interviews/truth-or-fiction-did-herod-really-slaughter-baby-boys-in-bethlehem.
33. Acts 1:6; even after Christ's resurrection, His disciples were still expecting some sort of temporal rule over Israel.
34. Matthew 5:17.

one's enemies and turning the other cheek, among many others) were indeed a revolution against the Jewish society's status quo. And it is a mistake to see these teachings as theological in nature only, as if they were limited to matters of belief, and not of action. Nor were they confined to the church, and not applied to government. In truth, the gospel is a template for living, not just a code of conduct for how adherents are to worship and what they are to believe. As will be explored later in the book, these teachings—and the actions they suggest are required—have profound implications for how we should treat one another, not just directly, but also indirectly through intermediary organizations and affiliations such as governments. God's commandments carry political implications that we ignore at our own spiritual peril.

Of course, the most notable contest between Jesus and the state comes toward the latter end of his mortal ministry, when Jewish leaders plotted to murder Jesus and hoped to trap Him to facilitate their evil desires.[35] For them, the grave sin of blasphemy was reason enough to punish Jesus. When brought before the Sanhedrin, the chief priests accusatorially asked Him "Art thou the Christ?"[36] Jews had been waiting for God's Anointed One to come yet rejected Him when standing in their midst. And when Jewish authorities were satisfied by Jesus's answer enough to levy punishment, they instead decided to offer Him up to the Romans. Obviously, Roman rulers did not care about the theological squabbles of their subjects, so the Jews conjured up political crimes instead, telling Pilate, the governor, that Jesus had been "perverting the nation, and forbidding to give tribute to Caesar, saying that he himself is Christ a King."[37] He was accused of disobeying and competing against Caesar, and Caesar permits no such competition.[38]

John records the interaction between Pilate and Jesus:

> Then Pilate entered into the judgment hall again, and called Jesus, and said unto him, Art thou the King of the Jews?
>
> Jesus answered him, Sayest thou this thing of thyself, or did others tell it thee of me?
>
> Pilate answered, Am I a Jew? Thine own nation and the chief priests have delivered thee unto me: what hast thou done?

35. Matthew 26:3–4; John 11:53.
36. Luke 22:66–71.
37. Luke 23:2.
38. The essential feature of the state is that it asserts a monopoly on violence—Caesar punishes those who aggress against others, but legally justifies his own aggressions.

> Jesus answered, My kingdom is not of this world: if my kingdom were of this world, then would my servants fight, that I should not be delivered to the Jews: but now is my kingdom not from hence.[39]

Pilate eventually returned to Christ's accusers, claiming to find no fault in Jesus, but the bloodthirsty Jews pushed back. "Shall I crucify your King?" Pilate asked them. The chief priests—the religious authorities of the time responsible for teaching and defending the gospel—remarkably replied: "We have no king but Caesar."[40] In one simple statement, the spiritually empty religious establishment sided with the state and against God. Jesus was ultimately killed in the common Roman practice of crucifixion. "This is Jesus King of the Jews,"[41] a sign above His head told onlookers, no doubt to demean and diminish the many claims made about Christ.

Later resurrected and returned to God's glory, Christ awaits His second coming and triumphant return. Christians look forward to that day when, during the Millennium, Jesus will rule as "King of Kings and Lord of Lords"[42] after an "end of all nations."[43] Of that day, we have been told:

> But, verily I say unto you that in time ye shall have no king nor ruler, for I will be your king and watch over you.
>
> Wherefore, hear my voice and follow me, and you shall be a free people, and ye shall have no laws but my laws when I come, for I am your lawgiver, and what can stay my hand?[44]

But what implications do Christ's teachings have regarding law before He returns? What can we learn from His comments about Caesar and submitting to authority? And what do modern Caesars look like, and how do they demand our loyalty?

All Hail Caesar?

The Roman occupation of Judea was just one of many conquests to which the children of Israel were subjected. Egypt, Assyria, Babylon, Persia, and Greece each took their turn claiming political authority over the children of Israel. During the time of Christ, the Romans were the occupiers,

---

39. John 18:33–36.
40. John 19:15.
41. Matthew 27:37.
42. Revelation 19:16.
43. Doctrine and Covenants 87:6.
44. Doctrine and Covenants 38:21–22.

and Caesar was the political authority. In modern times, Christians live in and are subject to a variety of governments and earthly rulers. And while Christ's mortal ministry reveals some commentary about Caesar that we will later explore, these references surely apply not just to the single political leader at the time of His ministry, but to political leaders generally. God's teachings before and after Christ's earthly life build an even stronger case for Christians to choose Him over the current Caesar of the day. Whatever the form of government we might live under as our "Caesar," there are bound to be a few common characteristics.

Caesar demands loyalty. Political leaders do not easily tolerate dissent. Early Christians struggling under the Roman occupation were targeted because their deity was seen as a rival monarch, a "king in direct conflict with the dictatorship of the emperor."[45] Caesar was deified and worshiped as the protector and provider of the empire. The idea of an invisible God assuming these titles obviously undermined the Roman leader's claims of legitimacy and might. Those who refused to praise the monarch were perceived as disloyal. The modern state, in contrast, does not demand our theological reverence; its demand for loyalty is religiously indifferent. One can believe whatever they wish about a higher power, but Caesar lays claim to earthly power. Caesar expects our financial tributes and personal compliance. And like a community that is expected (or happy) to support the local sports team merely because of where they live, Caesar expects those within his jurisdiction to bow the knee and confess his superiority because he is master of that geographical domain. All who live there are expected to be loyal and comply accordingly.

Caesar asserts divinity or divine support. Mortal men proclaiming themselves as god is nothing new. Political rulers have long asserted a claim to divine approbation and appointment. Egyptian pharaohs, Japanese emperors, Roman rulers, English kings, and modern-day rulers have all either claimed to be deity or claimed to have deity's support for their actions. Political rulers tend to appeal to and appear to appease the god or gods of the masses, leveraging people's religious feelings in support of Caesar's desired policies. By portraying himself a servant of God, Caesar can discourage dissent by encouraging the faithful to support his policies, since he allegedly shares their faith.

Caesar desires worship. Caesar is Christ's counterfeit; he replicates the worship of God to instead support the state. To be praised and given loyalty,

45. Scot McKnight and Joseph B. Modica, Jesus is Lord, *Caesar is Not: Evaluating Empire in New Testament Studies* (Downers Grove: InterVarsity Press, 2013), 46.

an alternative quasi-religious system is built for worshiping Caesar. Political temples and monuments (the Capitol, statues, Washington Monument, and so on) are erected for visitation and veneration. Rituals are created (voting, swearing into office) to encourage a shared political faith. Seminaries of learning (public schools and universities) ensure the rising generation learns what Caesar approves. Common prayers and hymns (the Pledge of Allegiance, the national anthem) cultivate fidelity and reverence. Sacred symbols and texts (the flag, the Constitution) are propagated to remind citizens of Caesar's greatness and presence—a shared identity for the masses who are affiliated with the state and its might. Like all great counterfeits, many people perceive these substitutions as legitimate and worthy of their devotion and support. "Abraham Lincoln used to say," remarked Rudy Giuliani, "that the test of your Americanism was . . . how much you believed in America. Because we're like a religion, really. A secular religion."[46] American Christians often cling to their flag as much as their Bible. "The name of the nation [has become] as holy as the name of God. The presidency is turning into a priesthood."[47] Caesar most desires worship because reverent subjects do not revolt; they see their subjugation as a worthy sacrifice.

Caesar refuses to answer to a higher power. As Christ's counterfeit, Caesar sees himself as the highest power in the earthly domain; he is the supposed sovereign, able to do as he pleases. And while superficially Caesar may claim to answer to or represent God, in reality Caesar asserts that he is a law unto himself. The state sanctions and excuses evil conduct that, if committed by a citizen, would be subject to swift punishment. Caesar plunders, controls, and kills people with impunity, confident that he can get away with it. Doctrines such as executive privilege and immunity ("the king can do no wrong") are invented to justify Caesar's actions and exempt him from accountability. They are evidence that he thinks himself a god.

Caesar offers protection from the enemy. The core function of government is to physically protect citizens from foreign threats and suppress domestic disturbances. Caesar is eager to offer this service and be seen as the people's protector, so they in turn praise him for all success in this regard. Caesar desires and claims to be the source of safety and security—and where enemies do not naturally exist, he manufacturers them. For as H.L. Mencken said, "The whole aim of practical politics is to keep the populace

---

46. "Text of Mayor Giuliani's Farewell Address," *The New York Times*, December 27, 2001, https://www.nytimes.com/2001/12/27/nyregion/text-of-mayor-giulianis-farewell-address.html.
47. George Monbiot, "America Is a Religion." Published in the *Guardian*, July 29, 2003; see https://www.monbiot.com/2003/07/29/america-is-a-religion/.

alarmed (and hence clamorous to be led to safety) by menacing it with an endless series of hobgoblins, all of them imaginary."[48] Caesar cultivates support and perpetuates his power by reminding the people of the dangers he says he is uniquely able to help them avoid.

Caesar uses coercion. Rome did not rule over much of Europe by asking nicely. Caesar constantly seeks more power—to expand dominion for greater control. Christ is "gentle and humble in heart,"[49] while Caesar is the antithesis of these virtues. The modern state is particularly violent and uses force to command respect, enforce its will, and suppress dissent. While Caesar prefers people voluntarily comply with his edicts and perceive them to be reasonable and right, he is not unwilling to employ coercion to get his way.

Caesar seeks the praise of the world. With pomp and circumstance, and public relations campaigns, Caesar widely proclaims his virtues and points to the grandeur of his projects. Whether building roads and public works, vanquishing a foe, or providing food or services to the masses, Caesar is egocentric and proud of his accomplishments—and he wants the world to know it. He is vain and competitive, seeking to aggrandize himself relative to other challengers.

There are many other characteristics we might assign to Caesar based on the historical record of fallen empires and modern nation states, but this list will suffice. To review:

- Caesar demands loyalty.
- Caesar asserts divinity or divine support.
- Caesar desires worship.
- Caesar refuses to answer to a higher power.
- Caesar offers protection from the enemy.
- Caesar uses coercion.
- Caesar seeks the praise of the world.

As we evaluate how Christians should act in relation to Caesar, these characteristics are important to remember. While Christians often study and ponder the attributes of Christ, they typically fail to contemplate Caesar's. This is akin to going to battle without doing any homework about one's enemy.

This enemy comes in many forms, which might cause Christians confusion, for if Jesus was referring to the Roman empire, how do his words relate to a modern republic? Do we apply his rebukes to North Korea, but not North Dakota? And since the empires of past millennia are vastly different

48. H.L. Mencken, *In Defense of Women* (1918).
49. Matthew 11:29.

from the modern nation state—including participatory democracies where "we the people" are supposedly in charge—does what Christ counseled even remain relevant? Yes, there exists a wide range of forms of government under which God's people have been ruled throughout history. From dictatorships to constitutional republics, Caesars come and go. But we can eliminate the confusion and consistently apply Christ's counsel by understanding the influence that manifests itself in each Caesar.

The Whore of All the Earth

After His baptism, Jesus spent forty days in the wilderness, "to be with God."[50] Led up to a high mountain, He was shown "all the kingdoms of the world and the glory of them."[51] Surely such a spectacular review of God's creations would be edifying and inspiring—a much needed spiritual boost for the Son of God before He began His ministry. In interruption, Satan arrived with a temptation: "All this power will I give thee, and the glory of them: for that is delivered unto me; and to whomsoever I will I give it. If thou therefore wilt worship me, all shall be thine."[52]

Cast down to this earthly domain, Lucifer sees earthly possessions as "delivered unto" him—and uses worldly treasures to finance efforts to reign on the earth. Adam's son Cain was the first to fall prey to Satan's promise that one can "murder and get gain,"[53] and then get away with it. Countless others throughout world history have similarly "entered into a covenant with Satan, after the manner of Cain."[54] This was Satan's offer to Jesus as well: "If thou therefore wilt worship me, all shall be thine." It is interesting to note that Jesus did not indicate that Satan was making an offer he could not fulfill; it was, perhaps, not an empty promise. In other words, it is within Satan's ability to influence those who desire and use power and wealth, and their allegiance can lead to action that Satan desires. Jesus did not call out his fallen brother for lying. He simply stated: "Get thee behind me, Satan: for it is written, Thou shalt worship the Lord thy God, and him only shalt thou serve."[55]

---

50. Joseph Smith Translation, Matthew 4:1.
51. Matthew 4:8.
52. Luke 4:6–7.
53. Moses 5:31.
54. Moses 5:49. See also Ether 8:22–23 and 11:15; this book will later explore the pervasive influence of secret combinations and how Christians must recognize and reject them.
55. Luke 4:8.

Lucifer's efforts did not spontaneously start once he was cast down; they are a continuation of the very reason for which he was cast down. Despite being "in authority in the presence of God" and "in the bosom of the Father" he was "thrust down from the presence of God"[56] for waging a full-blown assault against God's plan. "I will ascend into heaven," he said. "I will exalt my throne above the stars of God . . . I will be like the most High."[57] Lucifer's power play was to tell the Father that he would "redeem all mankind, that one soul shall not be lost, and surely I will do it; wherefore give me thine honor."[58] That honor was actually God's power,[59] and thus Lucifer's diabolical forgery was merely a deceitful attempt to increase his own power and prestige at God's expense.[60] This war in heaven resulted in Lucifer's expulsion down to the earthly domain in which he now operates. Since that time, God's children have wrestled against "principalities, against powers, against the rulers of the darkness of this world, against spiritual wickedness in high places."[61] Jesus recognized that Satan, for now, is the "prince of this world"[62]—the whore that has dominion over all the earth[63]—and the war against allegiance to God is still being fought. This prince "is in control, even in our own land. He is guiding the governments as far as the Lord will permit him."[64] Satan "sitteth to reign" in the hearts of those who rule the nations,[65] and those influenced by him "fill the judgment seats in many nations,"[66] offering their allegiance in exchange for wealth and power.

The true nature of these spiritual battles has been shared with several prophets. For example, the apostle John saw a detailed vision of the future, including many significant events.[67] Revelation's imagery illustrates a great battle between two churches[68]—or, rather, two distinct and differently minded

56. Doctrine and Covenants 76:25.
57. Isaiah 14:13–14.
58. Moses 4:1.
59. Doctrine and Covenants 29:36.
60. Moses 4:3.
61. Ephesians 6:12.
62. John 12:31.
63. 1 Nephi 14:11.
64. Joseph Fielding Smith, *Doctrines of Salvation*, vol. 3 (Salt Lake City: Bookcraft, 1954), 314–15.
65. Doctrine and Covenants 86:3.
66. Bruce R. McConkie, in *Conference Report*, Apr. 1980, 99.
67. Nephi was also given the same vision but was instructed not to document much of what he saw—that task fell to John (1 Nephi 14:24–28).
68. The Greek word *ekklesia*, and the Hebrew *qahal*, are both translated into modern language as "church" but are synonymous with "assembly"—a group of people

groups of people: the kingdom of God, and the kingdom of the devil. This divine duel unfolds with apocalyptic controversy in the pages of scripture. Unfortunately, John's writings are difficult to interpret, and thus difficult for many to apply to their modern circumstances. Though "plain and pure, and most precious and easy to the understanding of all men,"[69] when John had finished his task, a "great and abominable church" corrupted his words "that they might pervert the right ways of the Lord, that they might blind the eyes and harden the hearts of the children of men."[70] So who, or what, is this great and abominable church—the "whore of Babylon"?

Some religious leaders like Martin Luther and John Calvin have suggested that the evil force described in Revelation is the Roman Catholic church.[71] In contrast, one religious scholar argued, "No single known historical church, denomination, or set of believers meets all the requirements for the great and abominable church." He continued: "Rather, the role of Babylon has been played by many different agencies, ideologies, and churches in many different times."[72] But this vague interpretation of nameless and ever-changing actors is unsatisfying, for we cannot avoid a whore we do not recognize; we must know an enemy in order to defeat it.

Lucifer has been and continues to be that enemy. The whore persecutes and slays the saints,[73] seeks and uses wealth,[74] and has earthly dominion.[75] Nephi helps point out that the kingdom of the devil exists "to get gain . . . , to get power over the flesh, and . . . to become popular in the eyes of the world."[76] These are the characteristics of Caesar, and they are what the prince of this world offers. Indeed, we can substitute Caesar's name for the name of he who influences those who seek dominion over others:

- Satan demands loyalty.
- Satan asserts divinity or divine support.

---

gathered, but not necessarily for religious purposes.

69. 1 Nephi 14:23.

70. 1 Nephi 13:26–27.

71. "The Time Is Near," Catholic Answers, accessed December 27, 2019, https://www.catholic.com/magazine/print-edition/the-time-is-near. Elder Bruce R. McConkie shared this view and published it in his book, *Mormon Doctrine.*

72. Stephen E. Robinson, "Warring against the Saints of God," *Ensign*, January 1988, https://www.churchofjesuschrist.org/study/ensign/1988/01/warring-against-the-saints-of-god.

73. 1 Nephi 13:5; Revelation 17:6; Revelation 18:24.

74. 1 Nephi 13:7–8; Revelation 17:4; Revelation 18:3, 11–16.

75. 1 Nephi 14:11; Revelation 17:15, 18; Revelation 18:3, 23–24.

76. 1 Nephi 22:23.

- Satan desires worship.
- Satan refuses to answer to a higher power.
- Satan offers protection from the enemy.
- Satan uses coercion.
- Satan seeks the praise of the world.

God's fallen son demands allegiance.[77] He claims to be a god,[78] able to save us,[79] and thus demands we worship him,[80] just as he demanded of Jesus.[81] He perceives himself the ruler of this world[82]—the highest power. He creates a false impression of protection, lulling us away with the prospect of "carnal security."[83] He encourages murder and "all manner of secret works of darkness"[84] to get his way. He seeks for honor and praise.[85] And so, Caesar is Satan. Thus, the great contest is not between Christ and random rulers of earthly governments, but between Jehovah and Lucifer—the Son of God and the son of perdition. The war in heaven continues on earth today, and the prince of this world uses dictators and democratic rulers alike to pursue his ends.

With this context, it makes sense why Satan would seek to remove plain and precious parts of scripture that describe his activities, for an informed group of saints is better equipped to fight him and warn others to join them. We look to China with great alarm where Caesar is evidently forcing Christians to "adapt to socialist society" by retranslating scripture and injecting communist commentaries into the New Testament,[86] yet millions of Americans have passively accepted a similar precedent without even realizing it. The King James Version of the Bible is a product of similar Caesarean intervention; whereas the widely popular Geneva Bible contained commentaries and interpretations that educated the reader about concerns with political authority, the English Caesar at the time considered it "untrue, seditious, and savoring too much of dangerous and traitorous

---

77. Helaman 6:21–26.
78. Moses 1:19; 5:13.
79. Moses 4:1.
80. Moses 6:49.
81. Luke 4:7.
82. Luke 4:6.
83. 2 Nephi 28:21–22.
84. 2 Nephi 9:9.
85. Isaiah 14:13–14.
86. "China Trying to 'Rewrite the Bible,' Force Churches to Sing Communist Anthems," *The Christian Post*, accessed December 29, 2019, https://www.christianpost.com/news/china-trying-to-rewrite-the-bible-force-churches-sing-communist-anthems.html.

conceits."[87] For example, a marginal note in Exodus praised the defiance of Pharaoh to preserve baby Moses's life—an act worthy of one who follows God, but that cannot be tolerated by a competing Caesar. King James said of this note that "to disobey a king is not lawful" and that such "traitorous conceits should not go forth among the people."[88] So the government helped organize and fund the creation of an approved Bible that would deny the people these commentaries so as to continue cultivating the "divine right of kings" and corrupt combination of church and state. Many Christians continue to use this Caesar-approved set of scriptures today.

But true Christians cannot tolerate any such combination; we must renounce all affiliation with the kingdom of the devil. Membership in God's kingdom is exclusive and requires relinquishing membership in, and allegiance to, the enemy's kingdom. Thus we read that

> there are save two churches only; the one is the church of the Lamb of God, and the other is the church of the devil; wherefore, whoso belongeth not to the church of the Lamb of God belongeth to that great church, which is the mother of abominations; and she is the whore of all the earth.[89]

In other words, everyone who is not exclusively with the Lamb actually belongs to Satan's kingdom.[90] Additionally, membership in Christ's church does not mean that one is a member of God's kingdom.[91] Saints can unwittingly (or intentionally) be on Team Caesar, if they are not careful.

Christ is clear about this. In one parable, He tells of a field of wheat suddenly having tares—vexatious weeds—sprouting up among the crop. "An enemy hath done this," He said.[92] There are some among the wheat who are actually tares—"corruptions of the Church"[93] who profess membership in God's kingdom. These tares are contaminating the field until the harvest.

---

87. Cleland Boyd McAfee, *The Greatest English Classic: A Study of the King James Version of the Bible and its Influence on Life and Literature* (New York: Harper & Brothers Publishers, 1912), 53.
88. Ibid.
89. 1 Nephi 14:10.
90. Alma 5:39.
91. Robinson stated: "Just as there are Latter-day Saints who belong to the great and abominable church because of their loyalty to Satan and his life-style, so there are members of other churches who belong to the Lamb because of their loyalty to him and his life-style. Membership is based more on who has your heart than on who has your records." Robinson, "Warring against the Saints of God."
92. Matthew 13:24–30.
93. B.H. Roberts, ed., *History of The Church of Jesus Christ of Latter-day Saints*, vol. 2 (Salt Lake City: Deseret News, 1904), 267.

Similarly, and even more explicitly, the parable of the ten virgins points out that many who claim to be Christian do not sufficiently steer clear of the whore. All ten virgins received invitations to the marriage celebration, fully expecting to be allowed inside. Outwardly, they all appeared prepared and interested in the bridegroom—after all, they had gone through the motions of trimming their lamps once they had been notified of his arrival. But half of them were foolish and had not been sufficiently faithful. "Lord, Lord, open to us," they begged. The Lord simply replied: I know you not."[94] Jesus taught this same concept in the Sermon on the Mount:

> Not every one that saith unto me, Lord, Lord, shall enter into the kingdom of heaven; but he that doeth the will of my Father which is in heaven.
>
> Many will say to me in that day, Lord, Lord, have we not prophesied in thy name? and in thy name have cast out devils? and in thy name done many wonderful works?
>
> And then will I profess unto them, I never knew you: depart from me, ye that work iniquity.[95]

It is a sad but simple truth that many Christians support institutions and efforts sponsored by Satan. His global whore is comprised of whoever "fighteth against Zion," since, as God said, "they who are not for me are against me."[96] Who fights against God by competing against him for our allegiance? Who claims power to rule, and dominion over the earth? Who aims to dethrone God to exalt himself for our worship? Caesar.

This Is the Way

The followers Jesus attracted during his mortal ministry were not called Christians until years later in Antioch, as missionary work spread.[97] Previously, it appears that the manner of life practiced by disciples of Christ was simply called "the Way." As Jesus taught his flock about his impending return to heaven, Doubting Thomas said, "Lord, we know not whither thou goest; and how can we know the way?" Jesus replied, "I am the way."[98] This was taken at face value; the disciples came to understand that Christ's teachings were a set of instructions for returning to God's presence. Living

94. Matthew 25:1–13.
95. Matthew 7:21–23.
96. 2 Nephi 10:16.
97. Acts 11:26.
98. John 14:5–6.

how God taught was literally "the way" back to heaven. It is no surprise, then, that this is what the life Christ requires of us came to be called. Paul mentions that he previously persecuted "this Way"—those practicing this lifestyle—unto death.[99] Later, once converted to it, he sought after those who "belonged to the Way"[100] so that he might gather them to Jerusalem. As missionary work spread, "there arose a great disturbance about the Way."[101] Paul noted that the Jewish establishment considered "the Way" as "heresy,"[102] and Luke pointed out that the Roman governor at the time had a "knowledge of [the] Way."[103] Christianity is not a set of doctrines to be read about in books of scripture and superficially pondered in sporadic religious services. It is the way we ought to live.

The Way of Christ may look odd to the rest of the world; Caesar's followers are used to a different (and more popular) set of standards. Disciples of Jesus striving to be "in the world but not of the world" find themselves surrounded by a culture that enables and encourages the opposite of Christ's teachings. The dominant culture, comprised of a shared set of attitudes, values, and practices that promote the cult of Caesar, is the problem.[104]

God's people have long struggled to maintain a cohesive identity, and fidelity to God, while surrounded by cults. Time and again "they went a whoring after other gods, and bowed themselves unto them: they turned quickly out of the way which their fathers walked in."[105] But Christ's kingdom is essentially counter-*cult*ural—the true religion contrasted against the imposter cult and its would-be gods. Whereas Romans proclaimed their emperor as savior of the world and the prince of peace prior to Christ,[106] the disciples of Jesus appropriated these terms and applied them to the true Savior, for which Caesar was a mere counterfeit.

Jesus has set an example for us[107]—the Way we should follow. "That which ye have seen me do," He said, "even that shall ye do."[108] Like sheep,

99. Acts 22:4; New International Version.
100. Acts 9:2; New International Version.
101. Acts 19:23; New International Version.
102. Acts 24:14; New International Version.
103. Acts 24:22; New International Version.
104. Both terms, *cult* and *culture*, come from the same Latin root, which means to "grow."
105. Judges 2:17.
106. The imperial cult of Rome treated the emperor as a divine being—one to be worshiped and honored by his subjects. Caesar was showered with such titles as Savior of the World, Bringer of Peace, and Son of God.
107. 3 Nephi 18:16.
108. 3 Nephi 27:21.

we are to follow the Shepherd's Way.[109] More than mere actions to replicate, though, Christ's words leave would-be disciples with instructions which we must follow if we are to call ourselves disciples. Many profess "to know the Christ," yet "deny the more parts of his gospel."[110] What, then, does the gospel actually require of us that deviates from Caesar's cult and culture? If one were to follow "the Way" today, what would that look like?

These questions become easier to answer when considering an opposite question so we can know what to avoid: what do members of the "church of the devil" believe in and practice? After all, "if ye are not the sheep of the good shepherd, of what fold are ye? Behold, I say unto you, that the devil is your shepherd, and ye are of his fold."[111] The devil's core doctrine is what Lucifer has long sought for—to destroy the agency of man.[112] Since the "war in heaven,"[113] he has lusted after God's power. He fashions himself a god—the prince of this world[114]—and uses the earth's resources and our fallen nature to command and control as if he were God. As the great imitator[115] who desires to be God,[116] he promises power and wealth[117] to those who do his bidding. But more than that—he promises what mankind has always sought after: security and salvation.

How exactly did Satan seek to destroy our agency? The gift of moral agency—to choose for ourselves and receive the consequences of our actions—requires three things: options from which to choose, freedom to choose between them, and consequence for our choice. Like a three-legged stool, agency can be weakened or destroyed (in theory) by attacking any one of the three. Contrary to what some have thought,[118] Satan does not seek to force us to be righteous; no scripture mentions this being the case. Thus, Lucifer's premortal proposal that allured a third of God's children[119] included the ability for individuals to disobey God. He did not aim to

109. John 10:27.
110. 4 Nephi 1:27.
111. Alma 5:39.
112. Moses 4:3.
113. Revelation 12:7.
114. John 12:31.
115. James E. Faust, "The Great Imitator," *Ensign*, November 1987.
116. Isaiah 14:14.
117. Moses 5:31; 3 Nephi 6:15; Moses 6:15.
118. For more analysis of this position, see Connor Boyack, "A Widespread Misunderstanding About Satan's War on Agency," Connor's Conundrums, http://www.connorboyack.com/blog/a-widespread-misunderstanding-about-satans-war-on-agency.
119. Revelation 12:4; Doctrine and Covenants 29:36.

destroy agency by compelling only righteous behavior. Even Satan apparently recognized that mankind would need differing options and, accordingly, the freedom to choose between them. This is demonstrated further by Lucifer's claim to want to "redeem all mankind, that one soul shall not be lost." Redemption implies a deviation from what God requires; to redeem is to rescue from bondage or regain possession of what was lost.[120] This would not be necessary under a system of coerced obedience to God, since there would be no redemption needed from wrong choices; Lucifer therefore was not attempting to destroy agency by removing options to choose from, or the ability to choose them. These aspects of agency would remain intact even under Lucifer's suggested alternative to God's plan.

This then leaves the final component of agency: consequence for our choice. This is the "eat, drink, and be merry"[121] option that we see throughout scripture.[122] Deviating from God is justified as a "little sin" that will be overlooked; "at last we shall be saved in the kingdom of God," says the devil.[123] This was no doubt enticing to the premortal masses listening to Lucifer pitch a contrasting proposal. The ability to make whatever choice one wanted, and be saved nonetheless, was and remains tempting for many. Satan encourages people to follow him so they can do what they want to do and be held guiltless. It is the promise given to Cain,[124] and it is the offer that seduces all who belong to the devil's church.

God gave us agency so that we "may act in doctrine and principle pertaining to futurity" in order to "be accountable for [our] own sins in the day of judgment."[125] Just as a hired agent is accountable to his employer for the agency given him—say, for example, signing a contract or completing a series of tasks—we are accountable to God for the agency we are given in this life. We are to worship Him and glorify His name only. We are to rely upon Him for our security and salvation, and not the arm of flesh. He is our king, not Caesar. But the history of the world provides us with ample evidence that mankind repeatedly falls short of this standard; wicked people want to escape accountability for their actions, like a rogue agent who wants to avoid reporting to his master that he did not follow instructions.

---

120. See "Redeem," Webster's Dictionary 1828, accessed January 10, 2020, http://webstersdictionary1828.com/Dictionary/redeem.
121. 2 Nephi 28:8.
122. Several examples will be provided later in the book.
123. 2 Nephi 28:8.
124. Moses 5:30–31.
125. Doctrine and Covenants 101:78.

This, then, brings focus to Satan's efforts today. The goal is not merely encouraging people to be sinful—telling a lie, having an affair, stealing from someone, and so forth. Rather, he persuades people to commit evil acts in pursuit of power and wealth while deceiving them into believing they can do so without consequence. He undermines agency by leading the agent to believe that he has no master who will one day hold him to account—rejecting such accountability "in an attempt to sedate his conscience."[126] Rogue individuals, though, cannot dominate others without being held accountable. If you commit murder, chances are fairly certain you will be caught and imprisoned, and in some cases even executed. If you steal from others, they will sue you or call the police. If you try to physically control your neighbor's actions, he might physically push back in defense of your aggression. In short, a person who aims to coerce others will suffer the consequences.

But not if you represent Caesar.

Those who have the support—or control—of the state can "get away with murder," both figuratively and literally. They can command people to kill others, take their property, control their actions, and coerce them in all manner of ways. They do so without apparent consequence; Caesar is the god that controls the actions of mankind. The prince of the world orders people around as he pleases.

The state, then, is the institutionalization of consequence-free coercion. It is the mortal mechanism through which Satan encourages his followers to seek power and wealth at others' expense.[127] He says, through Caesar, that we can disobey God's commands and still be legally compliant, and therefore culturally accepted. Good is called evil, and evil good.[128] This satanic domination of government, present in our day, also existed in the past. It is the reason that at least two previous societies effectively imploded.[129] We

126. Lynn G. Robbins, "Be 100 Percent Responsible," BYU Devotional, August 22, 2017, https://speeches.byu.edu/talks/lynn-g-robbins/be-100-percent-responsible/.

127. "Those [two contending] forces are known and have been designated by different terms throughout the ages. 'In the beginning' they were known as Satan on the one hand, and Christ on the other . . . . In these days, they are called 'domination by the state,' on one hand, 'personal liberty,' on the other." David O. McKay, "Two Contending Forces," Brigham Young University, May 18, 1960.

128. Isaiah 5:20.

129. Both the Jaredite and the Nephite nations were destroyed because of the secret combinations of conspiring individuals who gained control of the government and oppressed God's people. See Helaman 2:13–14; Ether 8:21. These stories will be analyzed later in the book.

have been warned to avoid them in our day,[130] yet many Christians continue to support Caesar, and thus the satanic influences that follow.

The Way requires rejecting the counterfeit of Christ, and therefore renouncing any affiliation with the great and abominable church. As agents of God, the Way requires us to be held accountable for our actions, serving our King and doing whatever He has commanded. And as will be later discussed, Christ's teachings also suggest that the Way requires:

- Loyalty only to God, therefore no oaths or pledges of allegiance to Caesar in any fashion.
- Loving those who attack us, therefore not using military forces to wage war against them.
- Leadership through serving others, not exercising political power over them.
- Submission to true law, but not necessarily to whatever edicts a political authority may decree.
- Pursuing societal change through persuasion, not coercion.
- Rejecting the state, which institutionalizes coercion against others.

Ideas such as these are controversial for some, yet that is perhaps because we Christians have become such comfortable Caesareans that we are no longer practicing the Way. The Savior's words deserve to be taken seriously by those who claim to follow Him, yet we embrace the ones that are convenient while dancing around or altogether ignoring those that are culturally unpopular.

At the dawn of the restitution of all things,[131] God took stock of the state of affairs and had this sour note to sing about His children: "They seek not the Lord to establish his righteousness, but every man walketh in his own way, and after the image of his own god, whose image is in the likeness of the world, and whose substance is that of an idol."[132]

Satan is the prince of this world—the idol in whose image mortal counterfeits attempt to replace God. Caesar is the means through which he operates in this world. The state is the system through which he pursues his ancient agenda of corrupting God's people. He wants "to deceive and to blind men"[133] to the fact that they are members of his church—that they are flirting with the promise made to Cain,[134] and worshiping Caesar while attempting

130. Ether 8:23.
131. Acts 3:21.
132. Doctrine and Covenants 1:16.
133. Moses 4:4.
134. Moses 5:31.

to court Christ in the same breath. This is how Satan operates "under such perfect disguise that many do not recognize either him or his methods."[135] God was not referring to a world of atheists when describing those who "seek not the Lord." He described a largely Christian society that had become deceived by the prince of this world, and who had fashioned themselves a god in his likeness. This Caesarean corruption is how we worship idols without realizing it—not in overtly pagan fashion, with golden creations which we publicly praise, but by rejecting the Way of Christ. Like God's people long before us, we profess to follow Him while instead embracing the world's way.

"Wide is the gate, and broad is the way," Jesus taught, "that leadeth to destruction, and many there be which go in thereat."[136] This need not be our fate. Our agency allows us to choose the way we will pursue, but choose we must.

Two Masters, One Choice

After Christ's crucifixion, the Sadducees schemed how to snuff out the remainder of His subversive sect. "Let us straitly threaten them," they said, "that they speak henceforth to no man in [Christ's] name."[137] And that is what they did. But Peter and his fellow followers of the now-resurrected Lord continued defying the whore's demands to stop preaching and gathering; missionary work continued, as did the miracles. In response, the high priest and his fellow council members, part of the sociopolitical elite, "were filled with indignation" and ordered the religious renegades to be seized and imprisoned.[138]

After being released by an angel and continuing their ministry, the apostles were once again brought before the council. Peter was questioned as to why he had defied their threats. "Did not we straitly command you that ye should not teach in [Christ's] name?" Peter's response provides the theological foundation upon which Christians have defied Caesar in succeeding centuries: "We ought to obey God rather than men."[139] This continued a long tradition of fidelity to God despite defying the state: Moses's life was spared by such defiance,[140] and he later defied Pharaoh;[141] Jeremiah rebuked Jehoiakim;[142]

135. See *Messages of the First Presidency*, vol. 6 (Salt Lake City: Bookcraft, 1975), 179.
136. Matthew 7:13.
137. Acts 4:17.
138. Acts 5:17–18.
139. Acts 5:29.
140. Exodus 1:22; 2:2.
141. Exodus 7–10.
142. Jeremiah 22:13–19.

Mary and Joseph fled from Herod's murderous mandate;[143] Daniel rejected King Darius's anti-prayer decree;[144] Shadrach, Meshach, and Abednego chose God over Nebuchadnezzar;[145] and many other examples likewise affirm that worldly powers—wickedness encouraged and coordinated by the devil—fight against God. One scriptural story after another elevates prophetic heroes in the reader's eyes specifically because they rebelled against the Caesar of their day.

Those who would follow Christ must renounce the world and its prince. Jesus told His disciples that each person must "deny himself and take up his cross and follow me."[146] But what does it mean to take up His cross? It is to "deny [ourselves] all ungodliness, and every worldly lust."[147] We are to reject Christ's counterfeit and the mortal temptations of power and wealth that Caesar represents and utilizes. He then tells us to "forsake the world, and save your souls."[148] We cannot embrace Caesar and the satanic influences he manifests without corrupting ourselves. Following Jesus means leaving the world behind and avoiding all the related traditions and institutions that compete against Christ for our loyalty.

Both Christ and Caesar demand our allegiance. The great and abominable church—the great whore, or the organized oppression of men by one another through earthly rulers and political institutions—does not tolerate individuals who pledge allegiance to God and claim citizenship in His kingdom alone. And for all the praiseworthy examples from scripture cited earlier, there are also many failures. God's people have long been seduced by their various Caesars and often choose to flirt with the whore. In Christ's case, it was the establishment leadership—the chief priests—who called for His murder while in the same breath shouting, "We have no king but Caesar."[149] In earlier times, the children of Israel outright rejected[150] God by demanding a king so that they would "be like all the nations." They did not want God to be their protector; they preferred that His fallen prince be the one to "judge us, and go out before us, and fight our battles."[151] Samuel had warned them of what would come from embracing mortal rulers,[152] and

143. Matthew 2:13.
144. Daniel 6:7–10.
145. Daniel 3:4–6, 12.
146. Joseph Smith Translation, Matthew 16:25.
147. Joseph Smith Translation, Matthew 16:26.
148. Joseph Smith Translation, Matthew 16:29.
149. John 19:15
150. 1 Samuel 8:7.
151. 1 Samuel 8:5, 19–20.
152. 1 Samuel 8:11–18.

went so far as to call down "thunder and rain" to ruin their wheat harvest in order to demonstrate God's displeasure at their demands.[153] Prior to this, Israel attributed to Gideon, rather than God, their spectacular saving from the Midianates. To Gideon they said, "Rule thou over us, both thou, and thy son, and thy son's son also: for thou hast delivered us from the hand of Midian."[154] But Gideon refused, rightly rebuking them. "I will not rule over you, neither shall my son rule over you: the Lord shall rule over you."[155] But once Gideon died, his wicked son offered to fulfill their wish.[156] The would-be king murdered dozens of his siblings to eliminate their competing claims to his newly established throne, which the Israelites conferred on him.[157] Across the ocean, the new Jaredite settlement faced—and failed to resist—the same temptation. As the patriarchs prepared to die, they gathered their family together to inquire what they wanted of them. Perhaps unsurprisingly, given the trend, "the people desired of them that they should anoint one of their sons to be a king over them." This response was "grievous" to the patriarch prophets. The brother of Jared noted, as did Samuel to the children of Israel, "Surely this thing leadeth into captivity."[158]

The tension between Christ and his counterfeit is also demonstrated in the story of King Ahab, the unfaithful Caesar who corrupted the children of Israel by promoting the worship of the pagan god Baal in their community. He and his wife exterminated God's prophets in hopes of eliminating the competing faith.[159] Elijah, a prophet who evaded their murderous attacks, used God's power to bring a three-and-a-half year drought upon Israel in judgment for their wickedness.[160] Toward the end, he challenged Ahab in a prophetic duel at Mount Carmel to demonstrate the counterfeit nature of the Baal worship that plagued God's people. Four hundred fifty false prophets among the children of Israel converged, against the lone Elijah, to try to demonstrate their power. "How long halt ye between two opinions?" Elijah challenged them. "If the Lord be God, follow him: but if Baal, then follow him." He challenged the people to stop their polluted mixture of following both God and false idols.[161] Yet their response was revealing: "And

153. 1 Samuel 12:17.
154. Judges 8:22.
155. Judges 8:23.
156. Judges 9:1–2.
157. Judges 9:5–6.
158. Ether 6:22–23.
159. 1 Kings 18:13.
160. 1 Kings 17:1.
161. 1 and 2 Kings contains several examples of kings doing things that were "right in

the people answered him not a word."[162] Put differently, "the guilty taketh the truth to be hard, for it cutteth them to the very center."[163]

We may read such stories and feel proud of ourselves for avoiding pagan idols, but this is foolish; our society is as susceptible to supporting Satan, through his modern Caesars, as our brothers and sisters of old were susceptible to their Caesars' wiles. Dismissing the apparent naiveté of our predecessors is not only unproductive, but it may cause us to fail to recognize and reject current counterfeits. Indeed, the broad appeal of modern secular humanism,[164] in substance, if not in name, offers ample evidence that today's culture is just as guilty of chasing idols;[165] men continue to worship the work of their own hands.[166] The modern state is itself a counterfeit religion with its attending rituals, requisite sacrifices, scripture, authorities, seminaries, and more. The state is, and long has been, Satan's domain through which to tempt God's children to worship him. The effort to centralize power under political mediators is therefore a rejection of God.[167] Political power itself rests on distrust of God; we seek to do through the state that which we are unwilling to leave to God.

Just as righteous kings failed to tear down pagan sites of worship,[168] continuing to infect God's people, today many of us pursue a tainted worship of Christ that allows for and accommodates Caesar's influence in our lives. We pledge allegiance to both, constructing a syncretic religion that results in us drawing nigh unto God with our mouths, and honoring Him with our lips, while our hearts are far from Him.[169] God calls this "vain worship."[170] If more

---

the eyes of the Lord," yet these kings did not remove "the high places," a reference to pagan worship sites at which sacrifices were made and incense burnt. See, for example: 1 Kings 15:9–14; 22:41–43; 2 Kings 12:1–3; 14:1–4; 15:1–4; 15:32–35. The answer as to why otherwise righteous kings did not remove these sites may be that the religion had become so corrupted that the Israelites believed that Baal worship was one and the same with worshiping Jehovah; the religions had fused to accommodate the surrounding culture, of which the Israelites were a part. And on that basis, the Israelites had fallen into apostasy, despite believing themselves faithful. For additional analysis, see Stephen C. Perks, *Baal Worship: Ancient and Modern* (Taunton: Kuyper Foundation, 2010).

162. 1 Kings 18:21.

163. 1 Nephi 16:2.

164. Secular humanism is an atheist philosophy in which man is glorified as the author of his own destiny.

165. Doctrine and Covenants 1:16.

166. Isaiah 2:8; Micah 5:13; 2 Nephi 20:13.

167. As this book will later explore, the Book of Mormon provides ample evidence of this.

168. See footnote 190.

169. Matthew 15:8.

170. Matthew 15:9.

Christians rejected Caesar and abstained from participating in counterfeit statist practices, it is likely that those who worship in vain would look upon them with disdain and scorn. Just as prophets of old were ignored, attacked, or even killed for pointing out the corrupt religious beliefs of their community, those who follow the same course today are likely to be shunned by modern society—including those who profess to follow Christ.

While followers of the Way were "counted public enemies" because "they pay no vain, nor false, nor foolish honors to the emperor,"[171] modern Christians have been plagued by their collusion with Caesar. When we divorce Jesus from his revolutionary ideas on alternative social systems, we inevitably segment His teachings into different categories that we selectively adopt to fit our needs. Indeed, the temptation becomes to conform Jesus to our ideas rather than ours to His, leading Caesareans to imply a divine endorsement for their statist creeds; worship turns vain, and we "teach for doctrines the commandments of men."[172] It may happen subconsciously and unintentionally, but it happens all the same; Christ's counsel is ignored or warped to support war and violence, and the paternalistic control of one group of people by another. We seek after, and thus create, a god who endorses our idea on how the world ought to be run. Christ becomes a mere caricature, His teachings idolatrously intertwined with Caesar's to be culturally accommodating and appealing.

The scriptures are clear about this eternal contest, and one must choose sides.[173] We can either place our trust and have faith in God's law of love or in the coercive and human state—but not both. We either follow His commandments and rely upon Him to resolve our conflicts or we trust the arm of flesh[174] and praise mortal strength for our protection.[175] We are called to be "strangers and pilgrims"[176] in the world—not seduced into supporting its fallen prince. "No man can serve two masters," Jesus taught, "for either he will hate the one, and love the other; or else he will hold to the one, and despise the other."[177] We therefore must choose Jesus only—and not, as many do, be content with Christ with a side of Caesar. "Put away the gods

---

171. Tertullian, as quoted in *Ante-Nicene Christian Library: Translations of the Writings of the Fathers Down to A.D. 325*, vol XI (Edinburgh: T&T Clark, 1869), 113.
172. Ibid.
173. Revelation 3:16.
174. 2 Nephi 4:34; Jeremiah 17:5.
175. Deuteronomy 8.
176. 1 Peter 2:11.
177. Matthew 6:24; note that Mammon may also reference Caesar, because the coinage of the time bore his image and served to further deify him as a competing, idolatrous god.

which your fathers served," the prophet Joshua proclaimed to the children of Israel. "Choose you this day whom ye will serve."[178]

Between these two masters—Christ and His counterfeit—we must ultimately choose. But can we choose if we do not understand the choice? If we do not recognize the counterfeit, can we understand it? It is perhaps for this reason that, "with great earnestness," we should "waste and wear out our lives in bringing to light all the hidden things of darkness,"[179] in order to help others see and avoid the pitfalls that have plagued God's people for millennia. Many Christians continue to stumble "because they are taught by the precepts of men,"[180] as if "they are walking in darkness at noon-day"[181]—as good a description as any for Christians who fail to understand the problems with supporting Caesar. The faithful must shake off these chains[182] of ignorance, for we are commanded to "contend against . . . the church of the devil."[183] It is a fight of eternal importance, and befriending the enemy is not a winning strategy.

No more excuses. No more flirting with the whore and halting between two opinions. It is time for the followers of Christ to abandon their summer cottage in Babylon, shake off the statist counterfeit religion, and choose only Him.

178. Joshua 24:14–15.
179. Doctrine and Covenants 123:13–14.
180. 2 Nephi 28:14.
181. Doctrine and Covenants 95:6.
182. 2 Nephi 1:13.
183. Doctrine and Covenants 18:20; 84:117.

THE LAW OF LOVE

After centuries of attempting to adhere to the law of Moses, the core tenets of the Jewish faith had become corrupted on two fronts. On the one hand, there were idolatrous influences from neighboring cultures. On the other hand, certain factions like the Pharisees ignored the core tenets in favor of peripheral and superficial compliance with restrictive mandates, missing the theological forest for the trees. Among their many doctrinal debates, the Pharisees had tried to determine which of God's commandments were greatest by ranking and prioritizing them—ultimately in an effort to affirm their own righteousness. But this debate was difficult, as the group had identified more than 600 commandments.[1] If these austere

1. "The Rabbinical schools, in their meddling, carnal, superficial spirit of word-weaving and letter-worship, had spun large accumulations of worthless subtlety all over the Mosaic law. Among other things they had wasted their idleness in fantastic attempts to count, and classify, and weigh, and measure all the separate commandments of the ceremonial and moral law. They had come to the sapient conclusion that there were 248 affirmative precepts, being as many as the members in the human body, and 365 negative precepts, being as many as the arteries and veins, or the days of the year: the total being 613, which was also the number of letters in the decalog. They arrived at the same result from the fact that the Jews were commanded (Numbers 15:38) to wear fringes (*tsitsith*) on the corners of their *tallith*, bound with a thread of blue; and as each fringe had eight threads and five knots, and the letters of the word *tsitsith* make 600, the total number of commandments was, as before 613. Now surely, out of such a large number of precepts and prohibitions, *all* could not be of quite the same value; some were 'light' (*kal*), and some were 'heavy' (*kobhed*). But which? and what was the greatest commandment of all? According to some Rabbis, the most important of all is that about the *tephillin* and the *tsitsith*, the fringes and phylacteries; and 'he who diligently observes it is regarded in the same light as if he had kept the whole Law.'" From Frederic W. Farrar, *The Life of Christ* (Salt Lake City: Bookcraft,

religious scholars could not determine amongst themselves which of these many mandates deserved to be considered the greatest, then surely the son of a lowly carpenter from Galilee would be unable to provide an answer.

That must have been the thought going through the mind of the Pharisee who asked Jesus, "Master, which is the great commandment in the law?" Presumably, this was an attempt to try and trap Him in a doctrinal gotcha to prove His theological ignorance—and the Pharisee's superiority.

> Jesus said unto him, Thou shalt love the Lord thy God with all thy heart, and with all thy soul, and with all thy mind. This is the first and great commandment.
>
> And the second is like unto it, Thou shalt love thy neighbour as thyself. On these two commandments hang all the law and the prophets.[2]

Though the Law of Moses had been encumbered with numerous superficial and distracting dictates, God's chief commandment was already ancient. Jesus was not telling the Pharisees anything new. Reminding the children of Israel that they were once strangers in another land, God had long ago told them that "the stranger who resides with you shall be to you as one of your citizens; you shall love him as yourself, for you were strangers in the land of Egypt."[3] He also told them not to "take vengeance or bear a grudge against your kinsfolk. Love your neighbor as yourself."[4] Instead, Israelites rejected this counsel. By the time of Christ, they had become nationalistic and distrustful of so-called "strangers."

This was seen most clearly in the case of the Samaritans. The Samaritans were distant cousins of the Jews who, as a result of Assyrian and Babylonian conquest, were partly Israelite and partly gentile. A theological divide split the two communities until they became bitter opponents and antagonized one another.[5] Thus, when a lawyer conceded to Jesus that loving one's neighbor as oneself is required for eternal life, he attempted to justify his limited view of this law's application by asking Him, "Who is my neighbour?"[6] Jesus then gave the parable of the Good Samaritan,[7] illustrating that this reviled Samaritan man, who was considered by Jews to be impure and unworthy, was the good neighbor loving others as one's self.

1994), 528–29.
2. Matthew 22:36–40.
3. Leviticus 19:34; see also Exodus 22:20 and Deuteronomy 10:19.
4. Leviticus 19:18.
5. John 4:9.
6. Luke 10:25–29.
7. Luke 10:30–37.

It was he, not the Jewish priest or Levite, who had done the right thing in God's eyes. If a Samaritan could do this, Jesus was suggesting, then so can—and so should—a Jew. Perhaps to make the point even more clearly that loving one's neighbor included the despised Samaritans, and thus by extension, all of God's children, Jesus publicly revealed himself as Messiah not in the Jewish temple, nor among the religious elite in Jerusalem, but to an unworthy Samaritan woman[8] who was considered to be inherently unclean and taboo.

This law of love was so central to God's previous teachings that when Jesus taught it throughout His ministry,[9] He explained that "all the law and the prophets"[10] hang upon this gospel pillar. This term was a reference to Hebrew scripture, "the law" being the Torah, or the five books of Moses,[11] and "the prophets" being the subsequent prophets who followed, and their teachings in what is now called the Old Testament. Put differently, Christ was saying that everything these prophetic predecessors were teaching was centered on the principle of loving God and loving one's neighbor as one's self. This was clearly understood by His disciples; Paul taught, for example, that "all the law is fulfilled in one word, even in this: Thou shalt love thy neighbor as thyself."[12] One might argue that Jesus's ministry was intended in part to remove the religious fluff that had distracted His people and realign their focus on what was previously taught, but had been forgotten. Loving others is essential to worshiping God.

To Whom Does It Apply?

Many Christians appear to believe that the "Golden Rule," as it is commonly called, is only a mandate on individuals and not institutions—as if a loophole exists, providing cover from the commandment for organizations of people. But a group is composed of individuals to whom the law applies, so it therefore follows that it applies to groups of people as well. Forming a government, composed of individuals, does not magically make an asterisk appear after the scripture saying that God's counsel—upon which all of His law depends—is suddenly revoked.

---

8. John 4:5–29; verse 26 is the first instance in the New Testament in which Jesus says, "I am he," regarding His identity.
9. He also taught the principle in Matthew 7:12.
10. Matthew 22:40.
11. Genesis, Exodus, Leviticus, Numbers, and Deuteronomy.
12. Galatians 5:14.

"Wherever it is found and however it is expressed," one of Christ's apostles taught, "the Golden Rule encompasses the moral code of the kingdom of God. It forbids interference by one with the rights of another. It is equally binding upon nations, associations, and individuals."[13] Christians must reject Caesar because they are commanded to love others; Caesar's very existence and power is predicated on hatred and control of others. Even well-intentioned policies of and people serving in the state are part of a system that relies upon coercion of others; the system's existence, and its "Iron Rule" of the proverbial sword to enforce its edicts, cannot be reconciled with God's law of love.

Caesar violates this law in many ways, chief among them through war. Satan's minions "maketh war with the saints of God"[14] while also fighting amongst themselves.[15] Since the world began, he has had "great dominion among men, and raged in their hearts; and from thenceforth came wars and bloodshed; and a man's hand was against his own brother, in administering death."[16] War has filled 92 percent of the years in recorded history,[17] with hundreds of millions of people killed—to say nothing of the destruction, displacement, and suffering caused.

The "war on terror" is the most recent example in a long line of conflicts in which Satan "stirreth up the hearts of men to contend with anger, one with another."[18] The attacks on September 11, 2001, provoked a strong desire for retribution, and many Christians called for war on their foreign "neighbors" in response. This sentiment also played out locally in the form of nearly 600 attacks on Arabs and Muslims. For example:

> Five hundred furious people mobbed a Chicago-area mosque and refused to leave until they were forced out by police. A Pakistani grocer was murdered in Texas.
>
> A man on an anti-Arab rampage in Arizona fatally shot a gas station owner who was an Indian-born Sikh . . . [and] harassment and violence at mosques and in Arab-American neighborhoods continued for months.[19]

13. Russell M. Nelson, "Blessed Are the Peacemakers," *Ensign*, November 2002.
14. Doctrine and Covenants 76:29.
15. 1 Nephi 22:13.
16. Moses 6:15.
17. Chris Hedges, *What Every Person Should Know About War* (New York: Free Press, 2003), 1.
18. 3 Nephi 11:29.
19. "Reaction to 9/11," History.com, September 6, 2019, https://www.history.com/topics/21st-century/reaction-to-9-11.

Just a few weeks after the attacks, the United States military began its fight in Afghanistan. Ninety percent of Americans approved of these attacks "in retaliation" for 9/11.[20] The belligerent attitude was exemplified by President Bush, who told others, "Either you are with us or you are with the terrorists."[21] Those who objected to this hate-filled response were branded as terrorist sympathizers. Just a few months after 9/11, President Bush shifted the public's attention beyond Afghanistan, to identify Iraq, along with Iran and North Korea, as part of an "axis of evil."[22] Punitive sanctions against the Iraqi people were renewed and focused. Bush told world leaders at the United Nations General Assembly that Saddam Hussein's regime was a "grave and gathering danger" and failure to escalate tensions would make the UN "irrelevant."[23] Days after this speech, Bush pushed Congress to authorize him to use military force in Iraq, to expand the "war on terror." A bill was introduced on October 2, 2002. Polling at the time showed a majority of Americans favored expanding the war to eliminate Saddam Hussein.[24]

With this backdrop in mind, the apostolic counsel referenced above becomes especially interesting. A few days later, The Church of Jesus Christ of Latter-day Saints held its twice-yearly general conference. On Saturday afternoon, Russell M. Nelson delivered an address that any faithful Christian would consider gospel truth. He drew attention to our living in the last days, full of prophesied turmoil. He referenced our mandate to follow the Prince of Peace and noted that He taught, "Blessed are the peacemakers: for they shall be called the children of God."[25] Then-Elder Nelson next highlighted the Golden Rule, as previously mentioned, noting that it applies to nations as much as individuals. He rightly taught that the scriptures "condemn wars of aggression" and that despite conflict, "Peace is a prime priority that pleads for our pursuit." Of diplomacy in the post-9/11

---

20. "Public Overwhelmingly Backs Bush in Attacks on Afghanistan," Gallup, October 8, 2001, https://news.gallup.com/poll/4966/Public-Overwhelmingly-Backs-Bush-Attacks-Afghanistan.aspx.
21. "Transcript of President Bush's address," CNN, September 21, 2001, https://edition.cnn.com/2001/US/09/20/gen.bush.transcript/.
22. "Text of President Bush's 2002 State of the Union Address," *Washington Post*, January 29, 2002, https://www.washingtonpost.com/wp-srv/onpolitics/transcripts/sou012902.htm.
23. "Bush asks U.N. to end Iraq's 'grave, gathering danger'," *SFGate*, September 13, 2002, https://www.sfgate.com/news/article/Bush-asks-U-N-to-end-Iraq-s-grave-gathering-2770868.php.
24. "Top Ten Findings About Public Opinion and Iraq," Gallup, October 8, 2002, https://news.gallup.com/poll/6964/top-ten-findings-about-public-opinion-iraq.aspx.
25. Matthew 5:9.

world, he said that "Resolution of present political problems will require much patience and negotiation. The process would be enhanced greatly if pursued prayerfully." Elder Nelson unabashedly affirmed that Jesus Christ's teachings would bring actual and welcome peace:

> These prophecies of hope could materialize if leaders and citizens of nations would apply the teachings of Jesus Christ. Ours could then be an age of unparalleled peace and progress. Barbarism of the past would be buried. War with its horrors would be relegated to the realm of maudlin memory. Aims of nations would be mutually supportive. Peacemakers could lead in the art of arbitration, give relief to the needy, and bring hope to those who fear. Of such patriots, future generations would shout praises, and our Eternal God would pass judgments of glory.
>
> The hope of the world is the Prince of Peace—our Creator, Savior, Jehovah, and Judge. He offers us the good life, the abundant life, and eternal life. Peaceful—even prosperous—living can come to those who abide His precepts and follow His pathway to peace. This I declare to all the world.[26]

Concluding his remarks, Elder Nelson reminded us that God has commanded us to "renounce war and proclaim peace."[27] While objecting to aggressive war is part of the equation, it is only a part. We should also, he said, "follow after the things which make for peace. We should be personal peacemakers." These, he says, are the true patriots. And lip service is insufficient—"we should *live* by the Golden Rule."

Dissent from the buildup to war was rare at the time, so the backlash from mainstream media was unsurprising. The Associated Press published a brief report, stating that the "Mormon church issued a strong anti-war message . . . clearly referring to current hostilities in the Middle East."[28] One newspaper's headline announced Elder Nelson had "railed" against war,[29] despite his remarks expressing not a shred of anger or contention at all.

The Church was quick to respond—perhaps anticipating a public relations nightmare like the one that happened just five months later to the Dixie Chicks, when one of the band's members told an audience, "We do

26. Nelson, "Blessed Are the Peacemakers."
27. Doctrine and Covenants 98:16.
28. "LDS leaders issue anti-war statement," *Daily Herald*, October 6, 2002, https://www.heraldextra.com/news/lds-leaders-issue-anti-war-statement/article_9b19cbd8-b781-597c-85af-3ed1ffd045fb.html.
29. "Mormon church rails against war," *Spokesman-Review*, October 6, 2002, https://news.google.com/newspapers?nid=1314&dat=20021006&id=5LszAAAAIBAJ&sjid=rPIDAAAAIBAJ&pg=6758,3918474.

not want this war, this violence, and we're ashamed that the President of the United States is from Texas."[30] In that case, massive controversy erupted, boycotts ensued, sales tanked, radio stations stopped playing their music, and the band very quickly plummeted from red hot to has-been. Drowning in war propaganda, Americans were quick to demonize anybody who did not support the war. Of course, this was merely a successful implementation of a long-known strategy perhaps summed up best by Hermann Goering, one of the highest-ranking Nazis who survived the war and who was well versed in propaganda. The people "can always be brought to the bidding of the leaders," he remarked. "That is easy. All you have to do is tell them they are being attacked and denounce the pacifists for lack of patriotism and exposing the country to danger. It works the same way in any country."[31] Bush's demand for solidarity with his foreign policy decisions lest one be branded a terrorist sympathizer—followed suit.

One day after the conference ended, the Church's public relations division issued a media advisory, stating that some news outlets had "misinterpreted" the address and encouraging reporters and editors to "consider the full text."[32] The advisory emphasized a minor part of the text, in which Nelson cited the un-Christian, Caesarean position of the Church to "[urge] its members fully to render . . . loyalty to their country,"[33] including military service—even when fighting against others of their same faith. Notwithstanding this exception, Elder Nelson correctly condemned wars of aggression and justified war in cases of legitimate self-defense, all the while repeatedly emphasizing that peace is possible, peace is optimal, peace is what we should all be striving for—even (and especially) during the run-up to full blown military intervention. "We cannot fully love God without loving our neighbor," Nelson reminded us. "We cannot fully love our neighbor without loving God."[34]

The Associated Press issued a follow-up report titled, "Mormons Back Bush Middle East Policy," explaining the Church had "qualified" Nelson's remarks and "offered support for President Bush's policy in the Middle

30. "Flashback: The Dixie Chicks Are Ashamed of the President . . . Again," *Rolling Stone*, August 7, 2014, https://www.rollingstone.com/music/music-country/flashback-the-dixie-chicks-are-ashamed-of-the-president-again-80036/.

31. Gustav M. Gilbert, *Nuremberg Diary* (New York: Farrar, Straus, 1947), 279.

32. "Message of Peace Misinterpreted," The Church of Jesus Christ of Latter-day Saints, October 7, 2002, https://web.archive.org/web/20030203035754/http://www.lds.org/media2/letters/0,10599,1592-1,00.html.

33. Nelson, "Blessed Are the Peacemakers."

34. Nelson, "Blessed Are the Peacemakers."

East"[35] in the form of an editorial in the Church-owned *Deseret News*. That editorial, issued the following Wednesday, completely contradicted the substance of Elder Nelson's address. "Saddam Hussein and the threat he represents to the United States and her allies will not go away on his own," it read. "This time, the nation may well have to strike first." It concluded that "Americans have known they must face Saddam again sooner or later. It appears the time has come."[36]

This was a tragic failure and missed opportunity to boldly affirm Christ's teachings, even if unpopular with the bloodthirsty public, who was eager to go to war. The Church's backpedaling and the theologically barren op-ed in its newspaper completely undermined the power and potency of reminding countless Christians, who had been caught up in hoping to see their enemies killed, that the Golden Rule still applied to their modern day circumstances. Jesus did not back down when challenged,[37] even when confronted with a hostile majority—should we? "If ye will not abide in my covenant ye are not worthy of me," Jesus tells his modern-day disciples. Immediately after, he adds that we must, presumably as part of this covenant, "renounce war and proclaim peace."[38] We must do so because those affected by war are our neighbors, and we are called to love them. Caesar desires war—with its hoarding of resources, centralization of power, and destruction of God's children—and cultivates conditions whereby one group seeks to dominate or retaliate against another. Christians are commanded to break this cycle of violence and obey the law of love.

A similar example highlighting the unwillingness of many Christians to apply the Golden Rule to war comes from former congressman, Dr. Ron Paul. In January 2012, Dr. Paul joined other presidential candidates on stage in South Carolina for a debate. Surrounded by a group composed heavily of evangelical Christians, the candidates fielded questions on foreign policy. All but Ron Paul advocated increased military intervention. Newt Gingrich suggested that the approach to those he labeled "America's enemies" was, simply, "Kill them."[39] Mitt Romney doubled down on the comment. "Of course you take out our

35. "Mormons Back Bush Middle East Policy," Associated Press, October 10, 2002, https://wwrn.org/articles/5994/?&place=united-states§ion=christianity.
36. "A clear and simple case," *Deseret News*, October 9, 2002, https://www.deseret.com/2002/10/9/19682020/a-clear-and-simple-case.
37. For example, when charged with blasphemy—a "crime" for which capital punishment was mandated—the high priest demanded of Jesus, "Art thou the Christ, the Son of the Blessed?" His simple but direct response: "I am." See Mark 14:61–62.
38. Doctrine and Covenants 98:15–16.
39. "TRANSCRIPT: Fox News Channel & Wall Street Journal Debate in South Carolina," Fox News Insider, accessed February 15, 2020, https://2012election.procon.org/sourcefiles/Jan_16_2012_republican_debate.pdf.

enemies, wherever they are," he said. "These people declared war on us. They've killed Americans. We go anywhere they are, and we kill them."[40] To consistent applause, the barbaric call to invade, bomb, sanction, and occupy foreign lands was welcomed by this predominantly Christian crowd with open, eager arms. Dr. Paul invited the audience to consider a different approach to foreign policy, imagining what the policies they were cheering for might feel like if they were on the other end:

> If another country does to us what we do to others, we're not going to like it very much. So I would say that maybe we ought to consider a Golden Rule in foreign policy: Don't do to other nations what we don't want them to do to us.[41]

The audience erupted with boos at the mere mention of this most fundamental Christian concept and the suggestion that it be applied to the government's policies. Having Christians on stage and in the audience outright reject this foundational law, upon which all of God's law is predicated, is another example of how many supposed disciples "draw near [to God] with their mouth, and with their lips do honor [Him], but have removed their heart far from [Him]."[42] Caesar's methods are culturally preferred; the "natural man"[43] prefers to rely upon the "arm of flesh"[44] and its promise of security and retribution.

As a result, "we are, on the whole, an idolatrous people," one prophet noted, saying he was "appalled and frightened" at how poorly God's people were following His expectations. He continued:

> We are a warlike people, easily distracted from our assignment of preparing for the coming of the Lord. When enemies rise up, we commit vast resources to the fabrication of gods of stone and steel—ships, planes, missiles, fortifications—and depend on them for protection and deliverance. When threatened, we become anti-enemy instead of pro-kingdom of God; we train a man in the art of war and call him a patriot, thus, in the manner of Satan's counterfeit of true patriotism, perverting the Savior's teaching [to love others]."[45]

---

40. Ibid.
41. Ibid.
42. Isaiah 29:13.
43. Mosiah 3:19.
44. 2 Nephi 4:34; 28:31.
45. Spencer W. Kimball, "The False Gods We Worship," *Ensign*, June 1976, https://www.churchofjesuschrist.org/study/ensign/1976/06/the-false-gods-we-worship.

For too long, Christians have aligned themselves with Caesar to justify a systemic deviation from God's commandments, seemingly believing that loving one's neighbor applies only to non-governmental actions of an interpersonal nature. If God's people have utterly failed to apply His law of love to the most serious of Caesar's actions,[46] can we be expected to consistently apply it to more mundane and less visible violations?

Deeds, Not Just Words

Before reviewing some of Caesar's violations of the Golden Rule, it is important to address one theory of how God's law should be followed in the context of government. This theory is that the Golden Rule applies to our communications and not our actions—as if polite discourse is the goal, even if that discourse is about hurting, stealing from, or even killing others. The theory is demonstrated in the announcement of "Christians from a wide range of theological and political views" who "kicked off a year-long program to express their concern about the polarization in our country and affirm the need to apply Christian principles to our political discussions."[47]

Though this coalition of Christians aims to promote the "practical application of the Golden Rule," they limit themselves by focusing only on discussing "biblical teachings about how to treat people who disagree with them." They want to "promote the use of the Golden Rule in political discussions," though not in the actual policies and programs, and "emphasize Christian teachings about dignity, respect, and the need for civility."[48] One congressman, echoing this theory, proposed legislation to create a "National Day of Civility" and handed out wristbands that said, "Practice the GOLDEN RULE every day!" Regarding our communications with one another, he said, "we must strive to disagree without being disagreeable."[49]

46. God's law of war, which requires us to lift up a "standard of peace" against aggressors three times before being justified in fighting back, "is an ensample unto all people, saith the Lord your God, for justification before me." No modern war has followed this law, yet countless Christians support ungodly warmaking in spite of it. See Doctrine and Covenants 98:33–38.
47. "Golden Rule 2020: A Call for Dignity and Respect in Politics," Revive Civility, accessed February 17, 2020, https://www.revivecivility.org/golden-rule-2020-call-dignity-and-respect-politics-0.
48. Ibid.
49. "Crist, Johnson Lead on Bill Creating National Day of Civility," United States Congressman Charlie Crist, June 22, 2017, https://crist.house.gov/news/documentsingle.aspx?DocumentID=227.

This was his sole focus of the Golden Rule's application, despite the fact that this particular elected official routinely supports policies and programs that violate God's law of love.[50]

Years earlier, another group of Christians advanced a similar effort, launching the "Evoking Our Better Angels in Politics" initiative. The effort, again, was limited only to addressing incivility. A statement circulated for people's signatures and support highlighted the focus:

> As I seek to apply the Golden Rule to political discussions, some of the things I don't want to do are:
> - Use inflammatory words, or derogatory names.
> - Have an angry tone.
> - Make broad generalizations about individuals or groups.
> - Delight in the difficulty that others face.
> - Assault the character of others or falsely impugning [sic] their motives.
> - Question another person's faith or patriotism.
> - Demonize my political adversaries or describe them as enemies.[51]

These are certainly important things that Christians should avoid in our communications. It is hopefully obvious that disciples of the Savior should be respectful, loving, and supportive in our spoken and written words. Indeed, to scream angrily at another person is to manifest our true feelings toward them; we cannot really love a person we are shouting at or speaking ill about. But is that the extent of the Golden Rule? Did Christ's counsel really only apply to the way we communicate with others? God's law does not say, "Thou shalt speak to thy neighbour as thou wishes him to speak to thee." Communication should obviously be considered a component of the law, but it is not the totality of it. Christians who limit their practical application to this superficial level are missing the mark.

What the Golden Rule does say is to "love thy neighbour as thyself," suggesting a far more substantive application than focusing on verbal and written communication. Incivility is a concern, but a tyrant need not be vulgar and mean; one can oppress others while not using inflammatory words. You can be both kind and unloving to another person—for example,

---

50. It is beyond the scope of this book to point out this particular congressman's voting record as evidence of the claim, but suffice it to say that nearly all of his colleagues are similarly guilty of violating the Golden Rule as evidenced by their voting record. For examples, see the Freedom Index by *The New American* or the scorecards produced by FreedomWorks.

51. Ed Stetzer, "Faith and Politics: Living the Golden Rule," *Christianity Today*, July 23, 2014, https://www.christianitytoday.com/edstetzer/2014/july/faith-and-politics-living-golden-rule.html.

you can fail to help a person in need while smiling as you pass by them. In Christ's example of the Good Samaritan, He did not suggest that the unhelpful Jews were mean. They simply failed to love the person in need. They violated God's law, even if they were not being jerks about it.

The principle behind the Golden Rule is sometimes called the ethic of reciprocity, and it is found in nearly all major religions:

- Buddhism: "Hurt not others in ways that you yourself would find hurtful."
- Hinduism: "Do naught onto others what you would not have them do unto you."
- Confucianism: "Do not do to others what you would not like yourself."
- Islam: "No one of you is a believer until he desires for his brother that which he desires for himself."
- Judaism: "What is hateful to you, do not do to your fellowman."
- Taoism: "Regard your neighbor's gain as your gain, and your neighbor's loss as your own loss."[52]

What is unique about Jesus Christ's teaching is its proactive nature. Read once more each of these other teachings and you will see that they are generally negative instructions—they counsel a person to avoid bad behavior. Now read Christ's counsel: "all things whatsoever ye would that men should do to you, do ye even so to them."[53] We are taught to act—to "do" things—in order to comply with the commandment. It is not enough to isolate ourselves from others and merely abstain from being uncivil or uncharitable to others; a person "filled with the love of God . . . ranges through the whole world, anxious to bless the whole human race."[54]

The fundamental problem with Caesar is not that he is uncivil or encourages others to act this way. A civil Caesar is still a problem because it offers us an idolatrous substitution for God. Thus, the Golden Rule invites us to review and realign not just our thoughts and words, but our actions as well. If we wish to truly follow Christ, then we must ensure that our actions—including our involvement with Caesar—are aligned with Christ's counsel. The reason is simple: the Golden Rule condemns Caesar's system entirely, not just the behavior of those who participate in it.

---

52. See Jacob Neusner and Bruce Chilton, eds., *The Golden Rule: The Ethics of Reciprocity in World Religions* (New York: Continuum, 2008).
53. Matthew 7:12.
54. Joseph Smith, *Times and Seasons*, January 1, 1841, 258.

Institutionalized Lawbreaking

The state relies on a monopoly of force. Coercion, or the threat of it, is how Caesar enforces his decrees. This behavior is inconsistent with the Golden Rule, for no person would wish to be threatened by a friend or neighbor. Governments therefore perpetually violate God's law of love.

The key to following the Golden Rule is rather simple, though more difficult in practice: we cannot do—whether directly or indirectly through an organization—that which we would not want done to us. We do not love others through the state's mechanisms. Rather, these instruments are available for people to oppress and control others through the political process. This reveals a critical failure of Christians: they excuse behavior through the state that they would never condone personally. In other words, while faithful Christians would never think to steal money directly from their neighbor, very few of them consistently apply this to the state; many Christians support and vote for laws that take money from their neighbor and redistribute it to others, including themselves. While Caesar's penchant for making war is an obvious example of violating the Golden Rule, it is important to analyze and address more common and conventional examples, such as this one and others like it, so as to better understand why Christians must reject Caesar—and not merely his more egregious actions.

Susette Kelo's neighborhood in New London, Connecticut, fell on hard times in the 1990s after the local naval research facility closed down. Elected officials were hoping to bring more business to the area. They used eminent domain[55] to begin taking property from people in Susette's neighborhood to benefit Pfizer, a company looking to build a new facility on the land. Susette and a few neighbors challenged the seizure of their homes in a legal battle that escalated all the way to the US Supreme Court, which held in a 5-4 ruling that the city was allowed to take their homes and give the property to another company.[56] The city officials involved would surely have been irate if someone seized their own property, yet they enthusiastically used the state's power to seize others' property they desired to control.

Eminent domain is a rare occurrence, yet it serves as another example of how people do through the state that which they would not do themselves,

---

55. Eminent domain is a law that allows a government, or authorized private organization, to take ownership of another person's property for any purpose it deems necessary or beneficial. The US Constitution does not prohibit this practice, but merely requires that the previous owner be justly compensated.

56. *Kelo v. City of New London*, 545 U.S. 469 (2005).

or wish done to them by others. But individuals frequently avail themselves of the state's power to impose their preferences on others, outsourcing their control of their neighbors, rather than doing the dirty work themselves. Consider the case of an Airbnb in St. George, Utah. Through Airbnb, homeowners share unused space with short-term renters who are looking for an alternative to a costly or inconvenient hotel. Residents of St. George had long been split on the issue, leading to contentious city meetings whenever the topic was discussed. The result was a law banning the practice, prohibiting property owners from using their homes in this fashion.

When Stephen Palmer and his family rented out their basement, unaware they were violating the city's law, they were surprised to receive a threatening letter in the mail, informing them that they faced jail time and heavy fines if they did not stop. None of the Palmers' neighbors even knew about their rental activity or were bothered by it, including the unaware mayor who lived two doors down from them.[57] Would any of these neighbors personally use force to detain Mr. Palmer and incarcerate him? Clearly not. Would they support the police threatening them if they wanted to peaceably use their property in a way that elected officials had arbitrarily prohibited? Unlikely. And yet, the system is set up to facilitate this perpetual violation of the Golden Rule, institutionalizing the breaking of God's law.

Jesus told the man wondering how to "inherit eternal life" that he should "sell whatsoever thou hast, and give to the poor, and thou shalt have treasure in heaven."[58] That is what Arnold Abbott decided to do, creating the Love Thy Neighbor Fund in 1991 as a tribute to his late wife. The organization continued the important work Abbot and his wife had enjoyed doing together: feeding the homeless and supporting the needy. In November 2014, ninety-year-old Abbott began handing out plates of hot food to homeless people in a Florida park, as he had done many times before. But this time was different. An approaching policeman grabbed his arm and said, "Drop that plate right now," almost as if Abbott were holding a gun, he later remarked.[59] He was charged with violating the law for feeding the homeless—a law the city council had passed just a week prior. That law limited where feeding sites could be located and required those providing

57. "St. George Shutting Down Airbnb Providers," Libertas Institute, May 26, 2015, http://libertasutah.org/interview/st-george-shutting-down-airbnb-providers/.
58. Matthew 10:17–22.
59. Mike Clary, "Homeless Advocate, 90, Gets World Attention as Fort Lauderdale Tries to Stop His Outdoor Feedings," *Fort Lauderdale (FL) Sun Sentinel*, November 9, 2014, http://www.sun-sentinel.com/local/broward/fort-lauderdale/fl-homeless-advocate-abbot-profile- 20141107-story.html.

food to obtain a permit. It further required food providers to furnish portable toilets and hand-washing stations, and ensure food was maintained at precise temperatures. Abbott decided to ignore the law and continue his service, racking up four additional citations, each of which involved a fine of up to $500 and up to 60 days in jail. "It's ridiculous," he said. "The whole thing was designed to rid [the city] of its homeless. Police told me anyone who touches a pan . . . anyone who is involved, will be arrested."[60]

Many of God's children are content to control others indirectly through the state, using power that the prince of this world readily encourages others to employ. The tyranny of the majority thus restricts the actions of the minority, running roughshod over God's commandment to love others. Businesses are forced to close because others want to compel community quietness on Sunday. Artisans are forced to produce items for celebrations to which they object. Children are criminalized for operating lemonade stands without a permission slip. Those seeking peace are made to finance war through taxation. Families are forced to send their children to the state's schools. People are thrown in jail for medicinally using a plant God created.

Many examples are available, but the point by now should be clear: the Golden Rule requires us to reject Caesar and not support the state.[61] We cannot do through an intermediary institution that which we would not want done to us. Loving others is a voluntary act that must be freely and directly offered; control through the political process, by contrast, is a means to express enmity[62] against others. Caesar's system facilitates oppression and control. In the words of a famous economist, it is "that great fiction through which everybody endeavors to live at the expense of everybody else."[63] It is therefore structurally impossible for a system of this nature to abide by the Golden Rule; following the law of love necessitates a rejection of Caesar's self-proclaimed right to coerce his subjects.

---

60. Kevin Conlon and Catherine E. Shoichet, "90-year-old Florida Man Charged for Feeding Homeless People," CNN, November 5, 2014, http://www.cnn.com/2014/11/04/justice/florida-feeding-homeless-charges/index.html.

61. A later chapter will explore this in more detail.

62. Romans 8:7.

63. Frédéric Bastiat, *The Bastiat Collection, vol. 1* (Auburn: Ludwig von Mises Institute, 2007), 99.

SERMON ON THE MOUNT

At the beginning of His ministry, Jesus "went about all Galilee, teaching in their synagogues, and preaching the gospel of the kingdom."[1] Shortly after He began to select His disciples, "great multitudes of people"[2] commenced following Jesus. In what is now called the Sermon on the Mount—Christ's first major recorded teaching opportunity—Jesus taught the gospel to His disciples and an assembled crowd in significant detail, "as one having authority, and not as the scribes."[3] This is an important distinction that is purposefully stated in scripture. Whereas the Jews derived their authority from recognized sources and quoted ancient rabbis and accepted tradition, Jesus did no such thing. He did not quote any sources or cite previous rabbis. He spoke on His own authority, despite having none of the credentials of a teacher according to the customs of the time. Rather than a prophetic "Thus saith the Lord," Jesus affirmed the truth of His words by prefacing them with the implicitly powerful, "I say unto you." This was so remarkably different from the conventional rabbinical style of the day that it is of little wonder that "the people were astonished"[4] by what He said.

The Sermon on the Mount spans several topics and broadly covers how to live a life that is dedicated and pleasing to God. It contains essential

1. Matthew 4:23.
2. Matthew 4:25.
3. Matthew 7:29.
4. Matthew 7:28.

truths on how a disciple of Christ ought to live, a social standard to which we must aspire. Yes, we fall short of His expectations—it is impossible, for example, to "be ye therefore perfect"[5]—but our inability to consistently apply these doctrines is not a justification for ignoring them.

Any Christian should ponder and internalize all of the verses in this Sermon and consider how to apply the words to their own lives. In this book, however, we will review only the handful of teachings that have direct relevance to the question of how one should act in relation to Caesar.[6]

Resist Not Evil

Alice Marie Johnson was one of nine children born to a family in Mississippi. She married and had her first child when she was only fifteen years old, and despite opposition, continued attending high school to complete her graduation. She worked for FedEx for several years and had four more children before divorcing their father in 1989. Without financial support from her ex-husband, and as a single mother of five, Alice understandably struggled financially. She developed a gambling addiction, leading to bankruptcy and a home foreclosure. Without the ability to make ends meet and a support system to help, she became involved in drug dealing out of desperation.

Alice was arrested in 1993 for assisting in drug dealing, primarily using her phone to relay messages. She was convicted of several drug-related charges as well as money laundering. It was her first criminal conviction; she had no prior record. The judge sentenced her to life without the possibility of parole in prison, plus an additional twenty-five year sentence.

"It feels like I am sitting on death row," she once said. "Unless things change, I will never go home alive."[7]

There are over two million people currently in prisons throughout the United States—a 500 percent increase over the last four decades.[8] Nearly

5. Matthew 5:48.
6. The "Golden Rule" and Christ's counsel that "no man can serve two masters" were taught as part of the Sermon on the Mount, in Matthew 7:12 and 6:24, respectively. Because these teachings were discussed in previous chapters, they will not be discussed in this one.
7. "A Living Death: Life Without Parole for Nonviolent Offenses," ACLU, November 2013, https://www.aclu.org/report/living-death-life-without-parole-nonviolent-offenses. Fortunately for Alice, and unlike so many others who are in her situation, her sentence was commuted by President Donald Trump in June 2018.
8. "Fact Sheet: Trends in U.S. Corrections," The Sentencing Project, accessed February

five million more are on probation or parole.[9] The so-called "land of the free" is the world's leader in incarceration.[10] This is a result of a criminal "justice" system designed around an "eye for an eye" approach—a systemic model of retribution in which those who harm others, or simply defy Caesar's decrees, are punished. All subjects are compelled to finance the warehousing and maintenance of such persons. Victims of crime routinely call for Caesar's might to be brought to bear against the offender, especially in the case of murder, where it is common to see family members demand that the state's ultimate power, that of a sanctioned killing, be employed against the murderer.

The concept of *lex talionis*, or law of retaliation, is sanctioned in the Old Testament. "And if any mischief follow," the law said, "then thou shalt give life for life, eye for eye, tooth for tooth, hand for hand, foot for foot, burning for burning, wound for wound, stripe for stripe."[11] The "punishment that fits the crime" model persists in modern society, and Caesar readily employs violence to respond to violence. The Lord says that vengeance is His,[12] yet Caesar is quick to offer a satisfactory substitute.

Jewish leaders had built up all sorts of excuses for retribution under the Mosaic model, despite being told "They shalt not avenge, nor bear any grudge . . . but thou shalt love thy neighbour as thyself."[13] Thus, when Jesus aimed to correct this clerical teaching, He said "Ye have heard that it hath been said, An eye for an eye, and a tooth for a tooth." The scholars of the day were perpetuating this model . . . so Jesus overturned it:

> But I say unto you, That ye resist not evil: but whosoever shall smite thee on thy right cheek, turn to him the other also.
>
> And if any man will sue thee at the law, and take away thy coat, let him have thy cloak also.
>
> And whosoever shall compel thee to go a mile, go with him twain.

20, 2020, https://sentencingproject.org/wp-content/uploads/2016/01/Trends-in-US-Corrections.pdf.

9. "Correctional Populations in the United States, 2013," Bureau of Justice Statistics, December 2014, https://www.bjs.gov/content/pub/pdf/cpus13.pdf.

10. "Countries With the Highest Incarceration Rates," *U.S. News and World Report*, May 13, 2019, https://www.usnews.com/news/best-countries/articles/2019-05-13/10-countries-with-the-highest-incarceration-rates.

11. Exodus 21:23–25.

12. Romans 12:19; Hebrews 10:30; Mormon 3:15.

13. Leviticus 19:18.

> Give to him that asketh thee, and from him that would borrow of thee turn not thou away.[14]

Rather than returning violence in like measure, Christ commands us to "resist not evil." Simply put, two wrongs do not make a right. Christ wants us to cease the cycle of blowback, whereby each party feels justified in retaliating when one offense was made as retribution for a previous offense. An eye for an eye, the saying goes, eventually leaves the whole world blind. Or as an Arabic proverb says, "He who strikes the second blow starts the fight."[15] An attack (physical or otherwise) is a problem, but we compound that problem through retaliation, turning an isolated event into a cycle of contention.

The larger question presented by this teaching is whether, and to what extent, violence is justified to pursue justice.[16] After all, *lex talionis* exists as a framework to mete out justice against an offender. But Christ will have none of it. We are to not resist, or respond in kind to, the evil. Perhaps part of the reason is that a person who uses a weapon consents to its use by his opponent. If we object to violence but use it against our enemies, then how can we criticize its use by others?

This is no doubt a radical teaching, for Caesar embodies and employs institutionalized violence—and many Christians strongly support and participate in this system. Anyone who attacks Caesar, his supporters, his property, or his friends, is dealt with swiftly and harshly. It is a perceived weakness by the world to be attacked and not respond. But imagine, by way of contrast, how the response to 9/11 would have looked had the Christian majority in the United States demanded we follow Christ's counsel. No deployment of hundreds of thousands soldiers,[17] many of whom were injured, impacted with PTSD, or killed.[18] No spending several trillions of others' dollars, saddling future generations with more debt.[19] No forced dis-

---

14. Matthew 5:38–42.

15. Leonard E. Read, "Resist Not Evil," Foundation for Economic Education, September 1, 1970, https://fee.org/articles/resist-not-evil/.

16. Even worse is the punishment of non-violent offenders, where the punishment doesn't "fit the crime" and is worse than the alleged crime itself.

17. "We Will Never Know How Many U.S. Troops are Abroad," *Pacific Standard*, January 23, 2018, https://psmag.com/news/us-troops-abroad.

18. "Casualty Status," U.S. Department of Defense, accessed February 24, 2020, https://www.defense.gov/casualty.pdf.

19. "U.S. Has Spent Six Trillion Dollars on Wars that Killed Half a Million People Since 9/11, Report Says," *Newsweek*, November 14, 2018, https://www.newsweek.com/us-spent-six-trillion-wars-killed-half-million-1215588.

placement of millions of people[20] and no killing half a million more.[21] Has all of the chaos been worth it? Has it advanced God's love? Has it complied with His commandments? These questions tend to answer themselves rather simply when viewed through the lens of Jesus Christ's clear teachings.

Christians tend to readily abandon the counsel to "resist not evil" when it comes to the topic of war, for clear provocations by a foreign aggressor tend to invoke—and injure—a nationalist sense of pride and unity. These individuals embrace their affiliation with Caesar and find their identity in him. They therefore see as enemies those who are subjects of a foreign Caesar—those who are on a different team. Then comes the dehumanization and the propensity to fear, hate, and attack "the other."

But we are all God's children, and this behavior is repugnant to a loving Father on whose "team" we are all meant to be. God has given us a clear directive when it comes to war. We are to "renounce war and proclaim peace," even against someone who has attacked us—a reaffirmation of Christ's counsel to resist not evil.

> And again, this is the law that I gave unto mine ancients, that they should not go out unto battle against any nation, kindred, tongue, or people, save I, the Lord, commanded them.
>
> And if any nation, tongue, or people should proclaim war against them, they should first lift a standard of peace unto that people, nation, or tongue;
>
> And if that people did not accept the offering of peace, neither the second nor the third time, they should bring these testimonies before the Lord;
>
> Then I, the Lord, would give unto them a commandment, and justify them in going out to battle against that nation, tongue, or people.
>
> And I, the Lord, would fight their battles, and their children's battles, and their children's children's, until they had avenged themselves on all their enemies, to the third and fourth generation.
>
> Behold, this is an ensample unto all people, saith the Lord your God, for justification before me.[22]

---

20. "Refugees and Displacement in the Middle East," Carnegie Endowment for International Peace, March 29, 2017, https://carnegieendowment.org/2017/03/29/refugees-and-displacement-in-middle-east-pub-68479.
21. "It's Time for America to Reckon with the Staggering Death Toll of the Post-9/11 Wars," *The Intercept*, November 19, 2018, https://theintercept.com/2018/11/19/civilian-casualties-us-war-on-terror/.
22. Doctrine and Covenants 98:33–38.

"All people" are to follow this law of war, lifting a standard of peace during and in response to an attack. God really means it when He says to resist not evil:

> If men will smite you, or your families, once, and ye bear it patiently and revile not against them, neither seek revenge, ye shall be rewarded;
>
> But if ye bear it not patiently, it shall be accounted unto you as being meted out as a just measure unto you.
>
> And again, if your enemy shall smite you the second time, and you revile not against your enemy, and bear it patiently, your reward shall be an hundred-fold.
>
> And again, if he shall smite you the third time, and ye bear it patiently, your reward shall be doubled unto you four-fold;
>
> And these three testimonies shall stand against your enemy if he repent not, and shall not be blotted out.
>
> And now, verily I say unto you, if that enemy shall escape my vengeance, that he be not brought into judgment before me, then ye shall see to it that ye warn him in my name, that he come no more upon you, neither upon your family, even your children's children unto the third and fourth generation.[23]

The Lord's declaration in the Sermon on the Mount to not resist evil was accompanied by three examples. In the first, Jesus said that "whosoever shall smite thee on thy right cheek, turn to him the other also."[24] The conventional and superficial interpretation of this passage has been that pacifism is what God requires; we are to take a beating and not defend ourselves. But the cultural context behind this example sheds a different light on a more likely interpretation.

First consider why Jesus made mention of a specific cheek—He did not apply this teaching to the left cheek, only the right. In the ancient world, the left hand was considered unclean.[25] To strike an adversary on their right cheek, then, you would have to use your right hand—and the only way to do so would be with a backhanded slap. Such an assault indicates an insult, not a provocation for a fist fight. It was a typical way to reprimand someone considered inferior—master to slave, husband to wife, Roman to Jew. Suddenly Jesus is suggesting something different—not submission to abuse, and certainly not a fist swinging back in the other direction, but turning the cheek such that the person would have to respond to you as a social equal. It

23. Doctrine and Covenants 98:23–28.
24. Matthew 5:39
25. *The Encyclopedia Americana*, vol. 17 (Detroit: University of Michigan, 2002), 163.

is a directive to act in a way your attacker might least expect, by refusing to respond in like kind, but instead to force him to see you as his social equal.[26]

Indeed, Caesar's aggression relies on dehumanizing the enemy; warfare throughout history has typically been preceded by psychological manipulation, whereby people are encouraged to see their supposed enemy as subhuman and unworthy of life. Turning the other cheek, then, asserts our humanity to the attacker and compels them to reconsider their actions, without perpetuating violence by using it ourselves. The subsequent examples Jesus offers follow a similar pattern in asserting our humanity—and through it, perhaps, our divine parentage—against an oppressive creditor and an imperial occupier. Violent resistance does not change hearts and minds.

Put simply, we are to not return evil for evil—either directly or indirectly, through Caesar. Righteous ends do not justify evil means; a corrupt tree does not "bring forth good fruit."[27] What we do—the means we use—is what matters, even if we think ourselves justified otherwise. Rather than responding to evil with evil, we are counseled to act differently, affirm our humanity, and respond nonviolently to the problems around us—behavior that is completely inconsistent with Caesar's attitude and approach to societal problems.

Love Your Enemies

Immediately after the counsel to resist not evil, Jesus then cites another teaching of the rabbis of the time: "Ye have heard that it hath been said, Thou shalt love thy neighbour, and hate thine enemy."[28] While the Old Testament, as mentioned in the previous chapter, called for loving others,[29] many Jewish leaders had narrowly defined who one's "neighbor" was so as to justify hatred and opposition of others. The Roman historian Tacitus took notice of this, citing the insular nature of Jewish society, that they kept to their own customs and relationships with one another, to the point that "they regard the rest of mankind with all the hatred of enemies."[30]

Jesus refuted this narrow application of the command to love others. "But I say unto you, Love your enemies, bless them that curse you, do good to them that hate you, and pray for them which despitefully use you, and

26. Walter Wink, *Jesus and Nonviolence: A Third Way* (Minneapolis: Fortress Press, 2003), 16.
27. Matthew 7:18.
28. Matthew 5:43.
29. Leviticus 19:34; Exodus 22:20; and Deuteronomy 10:19.
30. "Modern Jewish History: Tacitus on the Jews," Jewish Virtual Library, accessed March 1, 2020, https://www.jewishvirtuallibrary.org/tacitus-on-the-jews-110-ce.

persecute you."[31] In the Jewish context, enemies were—as Tacitus noted—the gentilic "rest of mankind." Christ calls upon us to love those of another nation as much as our own countrymen; we are to treat those of another tribe as members of our own.

The separation of God's children into various factions—each subordinate and loyal to separate Caesars—encourages the violation of this commandment by leading to the natural production of "enemies" whose primary sin stems from being members of another arbitrary team. God's family is separated into different tribes, with cultural reinforcement that elevates one's own team above that of another, leading to reactions like hatred and jealousy or full blown assault and war. Consider one area where this division and discord is notably seen: immigration policy. In this area, people are often considered competitors, if not actual enemies, by virtue of their birth location—a threat to the locals with respect to employment opportunities, language, culture, or general way of life.

"Those who come hither are generally of the most ignorant stupid sort of their own nation."[32] This came from the pen of Benjamin Franklin regarding those of German descent. Alexander Hamilton similarly worried about immigrants who "tend to produce a heterogenous compound; to change and corrupt the national spirit; to complicate and confound public opinion; to introduce foreign propensities."[33] John Adams was so fearful of the influence of immigrants from France—with whom the government was fighting an undeclared war—that he pushed for, and signed into law as president, a set of odious laws that authorized him to imprison or expel from the country any person deemed "dangerous to the peace and safety of the United States."[34] Immigrants from a country that was at war with the United States were subject to being apprehended and deported.

The fearful sentiment behind that law later led to Executive Order 9066, in which Franklin D. Roosevelt enabled the military to execute the forcible internment of people of Japanese ancestry following the attack on Pearl Harbor. Within three months, 110,442 people of Japanese descent were

---

31. Matthew 5:44.
32. Edmund S. Morgan, ed. *Not Your Usual Founding Father: Selected Readings from Benjamin Franklin* (New Haven: Yale University, 2006), 162.
33. Carson Holloway and Bradford P. Wilson, eds., *The Political Writings of Alexander Hamilton*, vol. 2 (Cambridge: Cambridge University Press, 2017), 502.
34. "Alien and Sedition Acts," *Our Documents: 100 Milestone Documents from the National Archives* (New York: Oxford University Press, 2003), 49.

rounded up. More than two-thirds were US citizens.[35] They were forced to quickly sell or abandon their homes and possessions, leave their jobs, and be relocated to internment camps, scattered throughout the country. There were no allegations of actual disloyalty against any of these individuals, nor was there a legal remedy whereby they could appeal the deprivation of their property and liberty.

Policies such as these are predicated on fear and distrust. They reflect an ignorance that encourages dehumanization; we see the best of ourselves but entertain the worst about others. We "[behold] . . . the mote that is in [our] brother's eye, but [consider] not the beam that is in [our] own eye."[36] It becomes easy—and legally justified—to deprive others of opportunity and fellowship because they are different from us and therefore somehow deserving of less. But xenophobia and protectionism are not merely American problems. Indeed, one of the reasons why Jesus shared the parable of the Good Samaritan was to expand the narrow Jewish view of who was considered one's neighbor. The reviled Samaritans were outsiders and enemies to the Jews, but Christ corrected the rabbinical justification to hate them. Samaritans, too, were capable and deserving of love. The same applies to our perceived and actual enemies; Christ calls on us to love them. Our neighbors are not merely those we share a cultural connection with, but all God's children.

What does this have to do with Caesar? First, it is important to recognize that Caesar needs a jurisdiction; he is defined by the boundaries that empower him. He has his circle of influence, in which he claims control. His circle's arbitrary borders—often the result of conquest—of necessity exclude others. God loves His children equally and expects us to do the same, but Caesar desires victories that require the defeat of others. His desire for glory is defined by subordinating and separating others. Through Caesar's manipulation, the human family, each of us children of God, becomes separated and pitted against one another, sometimes passively, oftentimes aggressively.

Second, Caesar institutionalizes and legalizes the hatred of one's enemy. The existence of an enemy prompts two attacks by Caesar: psychological, in which the "enemies" are dehumanized and portrayed as deserving of attack;

---

35. U.S. Department of State, *Digest of International Law*, vol. 8 (Washington, D.C.: U.S. Government Printing Office, 1967), 149.
36. Matthew 7:3.

and physical, in which Caesar sanctions violence against others. In normal society, assaulting or killing another person is generally considered immoral and unjust, but it is encouraged and justified by Caesar against his enemies. The state thus serves as a vehicle for Christians to reject God's commandment to love their enemy.

Caesar also encourages pride. As God's children are separated into tribes, each wants to appear strong compared to the next. Christians begin rejecting Christ's counsel to be meek and humble[37] and instead become puffed up in the pride of their hearts.[38] Mitt Romney, for example, wrote a book called *No Apology: The Case for American Greatness*—in which he argued that "we have nothing to apologize for when the balance sheet of our contributions is weighed against whatever mistakes we have made."[39]

Jason Chaffetz, another patriotic Christian, said that we should "never, ever, ever" apologize for America.[40] Former Governor Sarah Palin similarly said that we "should never apologize for our country."[41] And George H.W. Bush said, when campaigning to be president, that "I'll never apologize for the United States. Ever. I don't care what the facts are."[42] Amazingly, then-Vice President Bush doubled down on his refusal to apologize for anything the country does shortly after a Navy missile destroyed an Iranian civilian airplane, killing all 290 passengers (including 66 children).[43] Caesar encourages immunity from his actions, based on the notion that "the king can do no wrong." Christian virtues such as contrition and unconditional love are rejected by Caesar and his supporters as a sign of weakness.

Enemies come in a spectrum of situations. Some are actual aggressors seeking to rob, harm, or kill us. Others are merely people like us, but who have chosen loyalty to a different Caesar. Then there are enemies within our own tribe who cause us problems. Whatever kind of enemy another person

---

37. Mosiah 3:19.
38. Alma 5:37; 2 Ne. 28:31; Isaiah 2:8; Helaman 12:5.
39. Mitt Romney, *No Apology: The Case for American Greatness* (New York: St. Martin's Press, 2010), 99.
40. Holly Richardson, Twitter @HollyontheHill, February 20, 2010, https://twitter.com/HollyontheHill/status/9388601480.
41. "Palin picnic marks beginning of the end," *Politico*, July 25, 2009, https://www.politico.com/story/2009/07/palin-picnic-marks-beginning-of-the-end-025408.
42. "'Kinder, gentler' and other George HW Bush quotes," CNBC, December 1, 2018, https://www.cnbc.com/2018/12/01/george-hw-bush-quotations.html.
43. "Iran Air Flight 655," Wikipedia, accessed July 20, 2020, https://en.wikipedia.org/wiki/Iran_Air_Flight_655.

may be, that person is our brother or sister, and we share a Heavenly Father. God has called us to love them all the same. Caesar encourages the opposite.

Beware False Prophets

Another relevant teaching Jesus shared in the Sermon on the Mount is to "beware of false prophets, which come to you in sheep's clothing, but inwardly they are ravening wolves."[44] His apostles later continued the warning; Paul said that "in the latter times some shall depart from the faith, giving heed to seducing spirits, and doctrines of devils,"[45] and that "after their own lusts shall they heap to themselves teachers, having itching ears" which will cause many to "turn away their ears from the truth."[46] Peter foretold "false teachers among [us], who privily shall bring in damnable heresies, even denying the Lord."[47] If possible, Jesus said, "they shall deceive the very elect."[48]

It is tempting to reduce this warning to the spiritual realm, as if false prophets are merely random religious crackpots who seek to gain a following, misleading their adherents into believing they speak for God and have a divine message to share. And it is true that these types of radical religious groups exist on the fringes of society, typically fading into obscurity as quickly as they emerge into public awareness. Some might even suggest that ministers and members of incorrect religions fall into this category, but keep in mind that Christ referred to "ravening wolves" deceptively disguising themselves as sheep. This is not about people with sincere, though incorrect, beliefs—it is about intentional deceit.

Paul pointed out the importance of following Christ and His chosen leaders by contrasting committed disciples against those who become "tossed to and fro, and carried about with every wind of doctrine, by the sleight of men, and cunning craftiness, whereby they lie in wait to deceive." The gospel of Jesus Christ, then, is about truth, and even temporal truths (political, economic, and so forth) have spiritual relevance.[49] Caesar, by way of contrast, relies upon deception,[50] and his deceit is not limited only to

44. Matthew 7:15.
45. 1 Timothy 4:1.
46. 2 Timothy 4:4.
47. 2 Peter 2:1.
48. Matthew 24:24.
49. Doctrine and Covenants 29:34.
50. Doctrine and Covenants 10:25; Jacob 7:18; Alma 30:53; Doctrine and Covenants 50:3; Moses 4:4.

spiritual matters. Satan's ultimate trick is for people to "call evil good, and good evil; [and] put darkness for light, and light for darkness."[51] He offers "carnal security" so people "will say: All is well in Zion" as he "cheateth their souls and leadeth them away carefully down to hell."[52] In doing so, he cultivates a complacency in which people do not realize and respond to the problems around them. He justifies as good behavior things that would be clearly perceived as evil if done individually: assault, theft, even murder. He portrays his coercive acts as compassionate, arguing that the allegedly good ends justify the aggressive means. He deceives Christ's followers into thinking they can support and collaborate with Caesar and still remain committed Christians.

We cannot confine God's warning of false prophets to the religious realm, on the lookout only for counterfeit Christs who claim to be our spiritual savior. This would be like watchmen on the tower looking only for men with slingshots attacking the wall, while failing to spot the army passing right through the gate.[53] Our defenses must be raised against "any concept or philosophy that says redemption, salvation, sanctification, justification, and all of the promised rewards can be gained in any way except that set forth by [Jesus Christ]."[54] Caesar offers a counterfeit salvation—a promise of protection from problems and cradle-to-grave support to save a person from their own mistakes or circumstances outside their control.

It is Caesar to whom people generally look when in need, seeking support from the paternalistic state rather than their Father. Government programs abound, forcing some people to support others and displacing voluntary charity and the interpersonal connections—and divine blessings—that come with it. Famine, disease, economic turmoil, war, and other temporal problems prompt people to turn to Caesar for a plan; he is their savior to help them weather whatever storms pass by. Indeed, false prophets do not just preach a fake religion; they come "under the label of politicians or of social planners or so-called economists, deceitful in their offerings of a kind of salvation which may come under such guise."[55]

Satan is the chief counterfeit seeking to replace God. He wants us to worship him. The various Caesars he controls extend the "arm of flesh"[56] to

51. Isaiah 5:20.
52. 2 Nephi 28:21.
53. Doctrine and Covenants 101:43–62.
54. Bruce R. McConkie, *The Millennial Messiah: The Second Coming of the Son of Man* (Salt Lake City: Deseret Book, 1982), 47–48.
55. Harold B. Lee, in Conference Report, October 1950, 129–32.
56. 2 Nephi 28:31; Jeremiah 17:5.

God's children, offering them a seductive alternative to idolize and depend on. As a result, the many who are called end up not being chosen, as they "are walking in darkness at noonday,"[57] ignoring the evidence of and support from God[58] and rejecting Him in favor of a counterfeit master. God's children become "blinded by the craftiness of men,"[59] aided by the intergenerational "tradition of their fathers"[60] that perpetuates support for Caesar. False prophets deceive so many because those who believe a counterfeit to be true persuade others to share their view.

Jesus noted that "every good tree bringeth forth good fruit, but a corrupt tree"—in this instance, Caesar and his counterfeit plan of saving mankind—"bringeth forth evil fruit."[61] Caesar's centrally planned programs are a type of satanic plan of salvation, whereby politicians and bureaucrats aim to design systems and situations in which people will be saved from themselves. As Lucifer himself offered in the premortal realm, his mortal minions continue to proclaim an alternative salvation—one that requires undermining man's agency by denying him the consequences of his actions. And the message continues to be popular, for people who commit errors are easily tempted to avoid suffering as a result. Thus, the false prophets among us do not just preach another religion—they establish political and economic bailouts and justifications whereby man can "eat, drink, and be merry"[62] without relying on or answering to God. Caesar is the consummate false prophet, a corrupt tree that only brings evil fruit.

Secret Alms

Research subjects in Oregon were each given $100 and then presented different scenarios for how they could help the poor with that money. At the same time, the subjects were having their brains scanned using functional magnetic resonance imaging to determine the personal impact of giving. In some scenarios the subject was allowed to choose whether to give the money to a local food bank, whereas in others they had the money taken from them and given to the same charity, resembling Caesar's coercive taxation-based welfare model. The brain scans showed very similar "reward" responses

57. Doctrine and Covenants 95:6.
58. Alma 30:44.
59. Doctrine and Covenants 123:12; Doctrine and Covenants 76:75.
60. Doctrine and Covenants 93:39.
61. Matthew 7: 17–18.
62. 2 Nephi 28:7–8.

whether they personally contributed to the needy or had the money taken from them for that purpose.[63]

The problem with this type of study is that it assesses the personal benefit and physiological response to the action of helping others: a dopamine stimulus that incentivizes desirable behavior. For some, the incentive is not dopamine, but an accounting benefit; a majority of people would decrease their charitable giving if it was no longer tax deductible.[64] In the Sermon on the Mount, Christ counseled us to consider charity outside the context of personal reward:

> Take heed that ye do not your alms before men, to be seen of them: otherwise ye have no reward of your Father which is in heaven.
>
> Therefore when thou doest thine alms, do not sound a trumpet before thee, as the hypocrites do in the synagogues and in the streets, that they may have glory of men. Verily I say unto you, They have their reward.
>
> But when thou doest alms, let not thy left hand know what thy right hand doeth:
>
> That thine alms may be in secret: and thy Father which seeth in secret himself shall reward thee openly.[65]

This teaching assumes that Christians will be giving alms. Our collective failure to sufficiently do so has sadly led to the creation of a welfare state,[66] which takes care of the needy by coercing everyone to give—while inefficiently distributing the money so that much less makes it to those for whom it was intended. And those who feel that Caesar is responsible to take care of the poor are less likely to do so on their own. Thus they do not give alms on top of what they are taxed for that purpose. But Christ's counsel does not absolve us of almsgiving just because Caesar takes money from us. The poor will always be with us,[67] and it is our obligation to help them directly—not indirectly through Caesar's corrupt welfare system that compels people to be charitable.

---

63. "The Surprising Relationship Between Taxes and Charitable Giving," *The Wall Street Journal*, December 12, 2015, https://www.wsj.com/articles/the-surprising-relationship-between-taxes-and-charitable-giving-1450062191.
64. Ibid.
65. Matthew 6:1–4.
66. "In scripture, we find vivid portrayals of the blessings that come from honoring true principles, as well as the tragedies that befall when individuals and civilizations discard them. Where scriptural truths are ignored or abandoned, the essential moral core of society disintegrates and decay is close behind. In time, nothing is left to sustain the institutions that sustain society." D. Todd Christofferson, *Ensign*, May 2010, 34.
67. John 12:8.

Treasure in heaven comes through giving to the poor,[68] but Caesar deceives many Christians by making them feel—as the brain scans apparently found—that they are accomplishing the same end goal. But the purpose of charity is not merely to feel good about ourselves or financially support the poor. It is to connect giver and receiver so both give gratitude to God. We find equality together when "[our] abundance may be a supply for their want, that their abundance also may be a supply for [our] want."[69] The poor often have, and share, a spiritual abundance that a giver of alms benefits from, as both praise the God who is the source of all we have. We miss these connections and charitable consequences when using Caesar's counterfeit program of helping the poor. Indeed, we must oppose the perception of these programs as a satisfactory method of helping the poor, and directly take on the task ourselves as commanded.

Oathmaking

Nearly three centuries after Christ's birth, a Roman soldier named Marcellus converted to the Way. As a newfound Christian, he determined—as did many others in the early days of the Church[70]—that military service was incompatible with his faith. During a banquet he arose, removed his military insignia, and told his colleagues, "I serve Jesus Christ the eternal King. I will no longer serve your emperors."[71] What happened next was predictable and swift. Caesar does not tolerate his subordinates demonstrating such disloyalty. Marcellus was beheaded.

There are several reasons why a soldier might struggle to be a faithful Christian—chief among them the swearing of an oath of loyalty. Enlisted members of the United States military swear that they will "obey the orders of the President of the United States and the orders of the officers appointed over me."[72] In the Weimar Republic before Hitler rose to power, soldiers sim-

68. Matthew 19:21.
69. 2 Corinthians 8:13–14.
70. See Ron Madson, "The Restoration of Conscientious Objection," in *Dialogue*, Winter 2018, accessed March 25, 2020, https://www.dialoguejournal.com/wp-content/uploads/sbi/articles/V51N04_6.pdf.
71. "Marcellus," in *Book of Saints* (1921), available on CatholicSaints.Info, Nov. 19, 2014, https://catholicsaints.info/book-of-saints-marcellus-30-october.
72. "United States Armed Forces oath of enlistment," Wikipedia, accessed March 25, 2020, https://en.wikipedia.org/wiki/United_States_Armed_Forces_oath_of_enlistment; one can "affirm" instead of swear but this does not substantively resolve the issue.

ilarly pledged to be "obedient to the Reich President and to my superiors."[73] Other countries have similar oaths. This makes sense, since Caesar's armed forces are authoritarian in nature and are predicated on the model of subordinates carrying out the orders they are assigned. Insubordination is therefore punished, as it destabilizes this model.

To "swear" is to promise something upon oath[74]—pledging one's word to be loyal when called upon. In the Sermon on the Mount, Jesus addressed this issue as follows:

> Again, ye have heard that it hath been said by them of old time, Thou shalt not forswear thyself, but shalt perform unto the Lord thine oaths:
>
> But I say unto you, Swear not at all; neither by heaven; for it is God's throne:
>
> Nor by the earth; for it is his footstool: neither by Jerusalem; for it is the city of the great King.
>
> Neither shalt thou swear by thy head, because thou canst not make one hair white or black.
>
> But let your communication be, Yea, yea; Nay, nay: for whatsoever is more than these cometh of evil.

Just as we cannot serve two masters,[75] we cannot swear to fallible men while remaining committed to God. The reason is simple—if we bind ourselves to another person and are told to do something that conflicts with what God has commanded, we have placed ourselves in an untenable predicament. We must remain solely subject to God's counsel, and not pledge ourselves to follow the acts of another.

This matter is not reserved for those in the military—it applies to all of us. For example, consider something that is indoctrinated into nearly every American from childhood: the Pledge of Allegiance. It is memorized and regurgitated daily, with millions of children pledging to something they do not understand, training them for a future in which, as adults, they will reaffirm their patriotic pledge unquestioningly. The pledge's creator, Francis Bellamy, argued in 1892 that "the training of citizens in the common knowledge and the common duties of citizenship belongs irrevocably to the State."[76] He drafted his pledge to be recited by the youth of the

73. "Hitler Oath," Wikipedia, accessed March 25, 2020, https://en.wikipedia.org/wiki/Hitler_oath.

74. "Swear," *American Dictionary of the English Language*, accessed March 25, 2020, http://webstersdictionary1828.com/Dictionary/swear.

75. Matthew 6:24.

76. *Eleventh Biennial Report of the Superintendent of Public Instruction of the State of*

time as a way of encouraging loyalty to the government. Modeled after the "loyalty oaths" imposed on Southerners after the war between the states a few decades earlier, Bellamy's pledge gained widespread adoption and eventually the support of Congress. Today's version has changed in minor ways but substantively remains the same.

Christians should pledge themselves only to God. To promise loyalty or pledge allegiance to any aspect of Caesar creates an unnecessary conflict between two competing masters.

Judge Not

In 1985, seventeen-year-old George Perrot was put on trial for raping a seventy-eight-year-old woman in Springfield, Massachusetts. There was no typical evidence to support George's guilt—no blood, no semen. No DNA test concluded it was him. Even the elderly victim testified that George did not look at all like her attacker. It was a single hair that moved the case forward, discovered by an FBI agent on the victim's bedsheet. The agent told jurors he was an expert in hair and textile fibers, and that hairs were distinctive to a well-trained eye. He spoke in scientific-sounding language about hair follicles and concluded that "in ten years, it is extremely rare I will have known hair samples from two different people I can't tell apart."[77] On the basis of this testimony, the jury convicted young George, leading to a thirty-year stint in prison.

George was completely innocent. The FBI made up the supposedly scientific arguments—and not just in George's case. In thousands of cases, judges and juries gave substantial weight to the testimony of false forensic analysis, imprisoning and even executing people as a result. The federal government acknowledged "that nearly every examiner in an elite FBI forensic unit gave flawed testimony in almost all trials in which they offered evidence against criminal defendants over more than a two-decade period before 2000."[78] At least thirty-three people whose cases involved this fake FBI analysis were sentenced to the death penalty. Nine of them were actually

---

Washington (Olympia: State Printer, 1892), 331.

77. "Thirty years in jail for a single hair: the FBI's 'mass disaster' of false conviction," *Guardian*, April 21, 2015, https://www.theguardian.com/us-news/2015/apr/21/fbi-jail-hair-mass-disaster-false-conviction.

78. "FBI admits flaws in hair analysis over decades," *The Washington Post*, April 18, 2015, http://www.washingtonpost.com/local/crime/fbi-overstated-forensic-hair-matches-in-nearly-all-criminal-trials-for-decades/2015/04/18/39c8d8c6-e515-11e4-b510-962fcfabc310_story.html.

executed and five died from other causes on death row. "We have potentially tens of thousands of convictions tainted by false evidence," the director of the Innocence Project said. "It's going to take a herculean effort to right the wrongs in these cases."[79]

This is one of countless examples in the criminal justice system of a country that purports to presume people innocent until actually proven guilty, yet has a dismal track record. Over 4 percent of defendants sentenced to death are later shown to be innocent—1 for every 25.[80] Even a 1 percent false conviction rate, when applied to the millions of cases involving incarceration, probation, and other punishments, leads to tens of thousands of injustices. Caesars in other countries, of course, often favor dictatorial power over due process; justice has been on "a negative slide toward weakening and stagnating rule of law around the world."[81] In some cases, the state is comprised of well-meaning, fallible people attempting to mete out justice to others when they themselves are guilty of wrongdoing.[82] In other cases, it is hostile people oppressing others through political power. Either way, the underlying concern remains the same: Caesar is not a perfect arbiter of justice.

The King James Version of the Bible quotes Jesus as saying that we are to "judge not, that ye be not judged."[83] This leads some earnest Christians to conclude that we should never judge others at all. But the inspired translation of the Bible points out that we are to "judge righteous judgement."[84] Noah Webster's 1828 dictionary clarifies that in this context, *righteous* means to be equitable and just.[85] It is therefore unrighteous—wicked and evil, one might say—to cause an injustice to occur, or to deal with someone unfairly and improperly. Our ability to follow Christ's commandment, then, requires us to only judge when we can do so correctly and fairly. Caesar is unable to do so, especially as it pertains to his use of capital punishment, which brings a life-ending finality to his judgment. The record is very clear that the state often instigates injustice, rather than ensuring its opposite.

---

79. "Thirty years in jail," *Guardian.*
80. "The staggering number of wrongful convictions in America," *The Washington Post,* July 24, 2015, https://www.washingtonpost.com/opinions/the-cost-of-convicting-the-innocent/2015/07/24/260fc3a2-1aae-11e5-93b7-5eddc056ad8a_story.html.
81. World Justice Project Rule of Law Index 2020, accessed March 30, 2020, https://worldjusticeproject.org/our-work/research-and-data/wjp-rule-law-index-2020.
82. Matthew 7:3–5.
83. Matthew 7:1–2.
84. Joseph Smith Translation, Matthew 7:1–2.
85. "Righteous," American Dictionary of the English Language, accessed March 30, 2020, http://webstersdictionary1828.com/Dictionary/righteous.

SUBMIT TO THE LAW?

Many Christians dance around the Golden Rule and the counsel given in the Sermon on the Mount. They do not apply it at all to modern government. Instead, many seem to segment their approach to life by compartmentalizing politics and religion, intent on ensuring that the one does not affect the other. But this runs counter to the plain language of Jesus's teachings that what God commands applies to every facet of our lives, including how we interact with one another indirectly through government.

If the government were to mandate something egregious, such as killing people based on their ethnicity or dictating whether a person can pray, then Christians would surely find this offensive enough to resist, citing Peter's rebuke to the Jewish government officials that "we ought to obey God rather than men."[1] These conflicts between Christ and Caesar are easy to resolve, but they are also extremely rare; few people are presented with such a dilemma. Instead, where Christians routinely fail is in applying the teachings of Jesus to more common—and popular—governmental practices, such as taxation, zoning laws, business regulations, or even war. Do Christians have a duty to submit to the law in all cases, barring some obvious and over-the-top conflict between Caesar's orders and Christ's commandments?

Based on a few misreadings of scripture, many sincere Christians misinterpret their duty to government and, as a result, believe that we are to

1. Acts 5:29.

be generally submissive and loyal to the Caesar under which we live. "We are to obey [Caesar] for the Lord's sake, in obedience to Him, and for His glory,"[2] one pastor argues, summarizing the position of his many peers. Another says, "So what does a Christian do in a society like ours? We obey, we submit, and we have nothing to fear from the authorities."[3] Yes, an exception is "when the government asks us to do something that is in direct disobedience to God's Word,"[4] but therein lies the problem: if we fail to understand when Caesar is in conflict with Christ, then the exception is meaningless, and we wrongly align ourselves with and submit to Caesar.

Caesar is, of course, very powerful, and people generally want to avoid provoking his wrath. So when a secret policeman for the Nazi government visited the headquarters of the German-Austrian Mission for The Church of Jesus Christ of Latter-day Saints[5] in September 1933, the mission president, Oliver Budge, responded accordingly. Budge was asked about the attitude of his religion toward the National Socialist government. He assured the police officer that members of his church "were living in keeping with their claims, namely, to place members of the church subject to Kings, Presidents, Rulers, Magistrates, in obeying, honoring, and sustaining the laws of the land."[6] After the visit, Budge doubled down. In a letter to the Gestapo, he explained that his church taught that believers should

> class themselves with the best citizens of the country, and to support, in the full sense of the word, the ordinances and laws of the town, the state, and the country in which they live . . . . [We] teach that the present party in power, and the laws governing the country, be supported by the members of the church.[7]

As will be explained, this is a false interpretation of what God has said, but it perpetuates the narrative that a good Christian submits to Caesar

---

2. "Submission to Civil Authorities," Bible.org, July 3, 2004, https://bible.org/seriespage/submission-civil-authorities-1-peter-213-17.
3. "Why Christians Submit to the Government," *Grace to You*, January 30, 2011, https://www.gty.org/library/sermons-library/80-364/why-christians-submit-to-the-government.
4. "What does the Bible say about government?," Got Questions, accessed March 30, 2020, https://www.gotquestions.org/Bible-government.html.
5. Hereafter referred to as "the restored Church of Jesus Christ" or "the Mormon church."
6. David Conley Nelson, *Moroni and the Swastika: Mormons in Nazi Germany* (Norman: University of Oklahoma Press, 2015), 93.
7. Ibid, 94–95.

without question. It cultivates complicity in Caesar's activities, while encouraging many to become involved in and proactively support them.

Contrast Budge's letter, which was consistent with the beliefs of fellow leaders of the restored Church of Jesus Christ, with a letter issued by the Jehovah's Witnesses:

> We have no interest in political affairs, but are wholly devoted to God's Kingdom under Christ his King. We will do no injury or harm to anyone. We would delight to dwell in peace and do good to all men, as we have opportunity, but since your government and its officers continue to attempt to force us to disobey the highest law of the universe, we are compelled to now give you notice that we, by His Grace, obey Jehovah God and fully trust him to deliver us from all oppression and oppressors.[8]

This letter codified the faith's practice of not saluting to Hitler or the swastika-adorned flag. They refused to participate in the militaristic labor corps and the military itself. While the Mormon congregations were seeking compromise and recognition to preserve peace, the Jehovah's Witnesses sought peace but without compromising with Caesar. For this, their religious services were criminalized, their members lost employment, and nearly half of their German members served terms in prisons or concentration camps. Several thousand died from their new conditions during incarceration, and over two hundred were executed. Meanwhile, members of the restored Church of Jesus Christ served in Hitler's military, saluted his flag, struck references to Israel from hymnals, prayers, and lesson manuals, and ceased participation in the Boy Scouts in favor of mandatory Hitler Youth membership.[9]

Clearly, having the Church sanction rebellion against an oppressive military machine would be unwise; organizational opposition to a ruthless political regime would bring swift and fatal retaliation, as it did with the Jehovah's Witnesses. However, while *institutional* defiance is strategically foolhardy, the question of *individual* defiance can be treated separately, and in that realm we must address whether God actually intends for each of his followers to follow Caesar's orders as part of their duty as committed

---

8. Ibid, 95.

9. Ibid, 97–98. For example, "When the Relief Society . . . published a manual that contained a lesson entitled, 'Christ and the Gathering of Israel,' the mission office instructed all local leaders to 'cut these pages out and paste the adjoining two together.' According to the wording of the accompanying memorandum, 'It is our belief that any subject even remotely connected with the Jewish race would be better unexpressed in Germany today.' "

and compliant Christians. Few will dispute the wisdom of strategy and the importance of picking one's battles. It does little good to an individual or to that individual's family, congregation, or others to put up a quick fight and be swiftly punished, or executed, by Caesar. It is perhaps for this reason that God stated, "this is wisdom, make unto yourselves friends with the mammon of unrighteousness, and they will not destroy you."[10] It follows the old adage of keeping your friends close and your enemies closer; there is a logistical benefit in not incurring the wrath of a powerful foe.

But while strategy should be considered, when and how should Christians resist the state? Before diving into the question of civil disobedience, and when a Christian might be justified—or required—to disobey Caesar, we first must analyze the arguments articulated in support of submitting to Caesar to better understand when, or if, they apply.

Romans 13

Imagine a servant of Christ arguing, "Love for the homeland must be greater than the love for the Church." Then imagine him doubling down to assert that "the law of the country is above [Christ's] law."[11] These words came from the mouth of Bishop John Fang Xingyao of the Catholic Church in China. They parallel words spoken by many ministers throughout history, especially when confronted by authoritarian regimes. It is why the majority of German Protestants, during the Nazi era, "identified themselves with the 'German Christian Movement' whose leaders expressed a desire to be 'an evangelical Church that is rooted in our nationhood.'"[12] It is the reason Christians who resist military conscription are criticized by their peers as being insufficiently loyal to Caesar. It is the basis for patriots attacking their fellow countrymen who oppose Caesar's wars, especially if said wars are purportedly being waged in defense of one's supposed freedoms, values, or way of life.

In short, Caesar and his supporters have often weaponized a frequently misinterpreted set of Bible verses to cultivate compliance and imply divine disapproval of disobedience. And many Christians have internalized this incorrect doctrine to believe, and argue to others, that

10. Doctrine and Covenants 82:22.
11. "Chinese bishop says Catholics must put 'love for homeland' first," *Catholic News Agency*, December 3, 2019, https://www.catholicnewsagency.com/news/chinese-bishop-says-catholics-must-put-love-for-homeland-first-53789.
12. Craig M. Watts, *Bowing Toward Babylon* (Eugene: Cascade Books, 2017), ix.

we are to "obey the powers that be" when said powers demand something of us. As one pastor said,

> It seems that every time someone such as myself attempts to encourage our Christian brothers and sisters to resist an unconstitutional or otherwise reprehensible government policy, we hear the retort, "What about Romans Chapter 13? We Christians must submit to government. Any government. Read your Bible, and leave me alone." Or words to that effect.[13]

Here are the verses in question from Paul's epistle to the Romans:

> Let every soul be subject unto the higher powers. For there is no power but of God: the powers that be are ordained of God.
>
> Whosoever therefore resisteth the power, resisteth the ordinance of God: and they that resist shall receive to themselves damnation.
>
> For rulers are not a terror to good works, but to the evil. Wilt thou then not be afraid of the power? do that which is good, and thou shalt have praise of the same:
>
> For he is the minister of God to thee for good. But if thou do that which is evil, be afraid; for he beareth not the sword in vain: for he is the minister of God, a revenger to execute wrath upon him that doeth evil.
>
> Wherefore ye must needs be subject, not only for wrath, but also for conscience sake.
>
> For for this cause pay ye tribute also: for they are God's ministers, attending continually upon this very thing.[14]

Taken out of context that is supplied by other scriptures, this apostolic counsel becomes a call to obey Caesar who (no matter how depraved he may be) is "ordained of God," with minions who are "God's ministers" that are only considered a terror by those who are "evil." And whoever resists this power—without apparent qualification—is also resisting "the ordinance of God" and, as a result, "receive to themselves damnation." It is no wonder why dictators and despots have long availed themselves of this contextually bankrupt interpretation. Sadly, many disciples of Christ have formed from these verses a general perception that God demands we obey whatever the government tells us to do, and that failure to do so is sin.

Did Paul truly imply that total submission to the state is required by God? This is extremely unlikely, since Paul was a student of scripture and

---

13. "Romans Chapter 13," LewRockwell.com, August 11, 2007, https://www.lewrockwell.com/2007/08/chuck-baldwin/the-myth-of-romans-13/.
14. Romans 13:1–6.

was familiar with plenty of situations in which a righteous person defied secular authority.[15] Moreover, Paul was himself attacked and arrested for acting contrary to Caesar's imperial edicts.[16] Christians will typically and correctly concede, then, that obedience is not required to "the higher powers"—translated as "governing authorities" in the New International Version of the Bible—when Caesar commands something that Christ prohibits. "Of course one's allegiance to his nation is always subservient to his loyalty to God," the conventional wisdom goes, "and whenever the two come into conflict, obedience to the Lord takes precedence."[17] But this qualifier is so exceptional that only in cases of egregious conduct do most Christians consider whether their support for Caesar is theologically problematic.

Sure, a good Christian should still pray, even if it is banned by the government. And a good Christian should refuse to steal from others even if commanded to do so. But how often do exceptional circumstances such as these occur? The reality is that Christ and Caesar come into conflict far more often than is generally believed, and it is in these matters where the misinterpretation of Paul's counsel causes problems. Should a Christian submit to having taxes taken from them to fund an unjust war? Should we refuse to operate a lemonade stand without a $200 permission slip from the county health department? Should we not take a casserole to a neighbor without first obtaining a food handler's permit? Should we send our children to Caesar's schools? Or what about using Caesar to steal from others to benefit our business or future retirement? Conflicts such as these are common, yet many Christians have ignored them and accommodated Caesar's culture in their modified worship, just as God's people have long embraced idolatrous identities as part of their own.

All the angst that these verses have caused Christians in centuries past stems not only from misinterpretation and lack of context, but also mistranslation. Further revelation clarifies and corrects which "higher powers" are being referenced, restoring the passage's original intent: "Let every soul be subject unto the higher powers. For there is no power *in the church* but of God."[18] Further, the payment of "tributes" is modified to be "consecrations" to God's ministers.[19] The entire controversy dissolves when it becomes clear

---

15. These will be reviewed later in this chapter.
16. Acts 16:19–24; 17:5–7.
17. "Is Taking an Oath in Court or Reciting the Pledge of Allegiance Forbidden?," *Christian Courier*, accessed March 30, 2020, https://www.christiancourier.com/articles/270-is-taking-an-oath-in-court-or-reciting-the-pledge-of-allegiance-forbidden.
18. Joseph Smith Translation Romans 13:1.
19. Joseph Smith Translation Romans 13:6.

that Paul is speaking about being subject to religious authority—ministers of Christ, rather than minions of Caesar.

A person who asserts that Romans 13 demands subservience to Caesar has to come to terms with Paul's own words in the same epistle. One chapter earlier, Paul counsels us to bless those who persecute us[20] and to not recompense evil for evil.[21] We are told to avoid vengeance,[22] which is the Lord's, and to overcome evil with good.[23] All of these are consistent with Christ's teachings of love and forgiveness, even and especially to our enemies. On the other hand, Caesar's very nature is to respond to evil with more evil; threats are his language of choice, and violence his basic behavior. Paul invites us not to participate in or subject ourselves cheerfully to these corruptions, but actually to avoid them entirely as Christ's teachings inherently require. We must overcome evil with good, and so side with Christ over Caesar.

Render unto Caesar

Another scripture that Christians routinely cite in support of Caesar is one where Jesus references him by name. Pharisees, seeking to trap Jesus, asked: "Is it lawful to give tribute unto Caesar, or not?" After reviewing the coin that bore Caesar's image, Christ's answer stumped them: "Render therefore unto Caesar the things which are Caesar's; and unto God the things that are God's."[24]

This was, of course, a loaded question. Roman occupiers had imposed a tax years earlier[25] that led to a revolt, led by Judas of Galilee.[26] He argued that "taxation was no better than an introduction to slavery," and "exhorted the nation to assert their liberty."[27] He and his followers recognized God alone as a ruler over Israel. The Roman response to tax resistance was predictable and brutal, but the resistance was merely an intermittent exposure of a deep philosophical, political, and theological issue: either God and His laws were

20. Romans 12:14.
21. Romans 12:17.
22. Romans 12:19.
23. Romans 12:21.
24. Matthew 22:15–22.
25. This refers to the census ordered by Rome for the purpose of ensuring that the Jews were paying the taxes required by Caesar Augustus. As we read in Luke 2, this tax census is the reason Joseph traveled with Mary to Bethlehem, where she gave birth to Jesus.
26. Acts 5:37.
27. Flavius Josephus, *The Works of Flavius Josephus* (London: Joseph Smith, 1839), 483.

supreme, or Caesar and his laws were. These two forces were irreconcilably opposed, and faithful Jews bristled against Roman occupation as a result. They were being compelled to comply with Caesar, despite not recognizing him as a valid authority. Taxation was a recurring reminder of Caesar's counterfeit claims to power over God's people. And at the time, Jerusalem was a veritable hotbed of political and religious conflict. It is against this contentious background that Christ was asked the question about giving tribute to Caesar.[28]

It is important to note that the question was not just loaded; it was also a trap. If Jesus had answered that it was indeed lawful to pay tribute to Caesar, He would have immediately alienated the disciples who had just proclaimed Him King upon His entrance into Jerusalem. Some of His supporters no doubt included the Zealots who agitated against Roman rule and would have considered possession and use of a Roman coin to be a violation of Mosaic Law. Had Jesus instead answered that it was unlawful to pay tribute, then the Roman occupiers would no doubt have classified Him as part of the ongoing tax revolts they were swiftly shutting down and expedited His eventual execution. The binary options presented by the Pharisees led to problems no matter how the question was answered, and that is why they deviously crafted it the way they did. (It is also likely why Jesus did not give them the direct answer they sought.)

The question also suggests that Jesus had somehow led His followers, or the broader public, to believe that He opposed paying tribute to Rome—else why ask the question in the first place? That He might even entertain the idea of the tribute's unlawfulness suggests that Jesus seemed at least sympathetic to, if not supportive of, the idea. Yet, there was a strategic danger of being vocal and open about the issue, especially to accusers eagerly laying a trap to "catch [Christ] in his words."[29] Simply put, the Pharisees saw Christ's rejection of the tribute as a likely answer, which is why the trap existed in the first place.

The coin itself was an effective piece of Roman propaganda, bearing the image of Caesar "crowned with the laurels of victory and divinity"—surrounded with the words "Tiberius Caesar, Worshipful Son of the God, Augustus."[30] Coins such as these were a popular medium to reinforce the

---

28. The issue of paying tribute to Caesar followed Jesus to His execution; the assembled crowd accused Him of "forbidding to give tribute to Caesar," encouraging Pilate to kill Him. (See Luke 23:2.)
29. Mark 12:13.
30. "Render Unto Caesar: A Most Misunderstood New Testament Passage," Ludwig

cult of emperor worship and further the claim of Caesar's sovereignty. By offering the coin in the temple—the location of this exchange—the Pharisees were exposed for their religious hypocrisy by "bringing a potentially profane item, the coin of a pagan, into the sacred space of the temple."[31] If the Pharisees actually believed what they were inferring with their question—that Mosaic Law was superior to Roman law—then they would not have had the "tribute money"[32] in their possession to provide Jesus upon His request.

It is one thing to focus on the coin itself—an idolatrous object that would have caused concern for any faithful Jew. The real meat of the question, however, is found in the tension between Christ and Caesar and their competing claims of authority. When Jesus answered that we ought to render[33] unto Caesar what is his, and unto God what is His, what does that mean? What is actually Caesar's? Narrowly speaking, one might argue that the coin itself was the emperor's property. It was used by him to pay for people working in and helping the government, and it was used by his subjects to pay tribute to him. An object that bore the mark of an individual denoted ownership by that individual. Perhaps, then, Christ simply meant that the coin itself was imperial property and therefore should be paid back to Caesar upon demand (as in the case of taxes). Modern money is also minted and authorized by the government, so is Jesus simply saying here that we should pay taxes because the physical money we pay with belongs to the state?

The eternal tension between Christ and Caesar strongly suggests that His statement is about more than mere money or the clash for control between Jerusalem and Rome. All things belong to[34] and are beneath[35] God.

---

von Mises Institute, July 3, 2018, https://mises.org/wire/render-unto-caesar-most-misunderstood-new-testament-passage; some scholars have suggested that the Tiberius coin was not in common circulation in Judaea during Jesus's lifetime. If true, then the likely coin had Tiberius on one side and Augustus on the other—still bearing the image of Caesar. See Peter Lewis and Ron Bolden, *The Pocket Guide to St. Paul: Coins Encountered by the Apostle on His Travels* (Kent Town: Wakefield Press, 2002), 19.

31. Ibid.

32. Mathew 22:19.

33. *Render* means to return or pay back. See "Render," American Dictionary of the English Language, accessed March 30, 2020, http://webstersdictionary1828.com/Dictionary/render.

34. Leviticus 25:23; Deuteronomy 10:14; 1 Corinthians 10:26; Psalm 24:1; Doctrine and Covenants 104:14–15; 38:39.

35. 1 Chronicles 29:12–16; Psalm 47:2; 2 Chronicles 20:6; John 17:2; Doctrine and Covenants 63:59.

We are mere stewards of what is actually God's.[36] And yet Caesar claims jurisdiction and ownership of wide swaths of land and large segments of society. This is why Jesus asked his interrogators about the Caesarean "image and inscription" on the tribute coin, no doubt to remind them that God is owed exclusive allegiance and love and worship.[37] By suggesting that they render unto Caesar and God what belongs to each, Christ flipped the question into a challenge, inviting them to act according to their allegiances. Do they submit to, reverence, and support Caesar? Or are they faithful to God above all else? In the tension between two masters, whom do they align with? More to the point, who do *we* align with?

Caesar owns and lawfully controls nothing, so it therefore follows that we are not obligated to "render" anything "unto Caesar" since nothing actually belongs or is subject to him. Our allegiance and loyalty must lie only with Christ. Of course, as a counterfeit, Caesar contends that he has authority over us. Pilate, for example, asserted that he had "power to crucify" Christ. Jesus responded that "Thou couldest have no power at all against me, except it were given thee from above."[38] The state lacks inherent authority and therefore our obligations to it are not inherent and divinely mandated. Whether there may be strategic prudence to abide by Caesar's demands to a point, so as to be left alone so one can continue to ignore Caesar and focus on Christ, is an entirely different question.

The conventional wisdom that God demands submission to and support for Caesar is not justified by Christ's response to the Pharisees. In fact, the opposite is true: by rendering unto God, we honor Him and keep His commandments. We love others and follow the Golden Rule. We do not trespass against others. The state, of course, violates these requirements; Caesar, as counterfeit, cannot comply with Christ's counsel to love others. For this reason, rendering unto God demands that we reject Caesar.

The Constitution

Christians, particularly in America, are prone to regurgitate an apparent obligation to obey "the law of the land"—and in the case of the US Constitution, the "supreme law of the land."[39] We are told to "strictly obey every law of God, including the constitutional laws of the land in which

36. Doctrine and Covenants 104:55–56; 78:22; 136:27.
37. Exodus 20:4.
38. John 19:11.
39. Article VI, US Constitution.

[we live],"[40] but this raises problems for the committed Christian. What if Caesar's constitution contradicts Christ's counsel? And does every edict from Caesar become the "law of the land" we are divinely obligated to obey?

The Lord has said that we are "justified" in "befriending that law which is the constitutional law of the land."[41] Further, we are told not to "break the laws of the land, for he that keepeth the laws of God hath no need to break the laws of the land."[42] But this raises the question: are the laws of God always in harmony with the laws of the land? The term itself has been commonly used but little understood.

Most people seem to believe that "the laws of the land" are whatever Caesar has mandated. "Whether we agree with the [immigration] process or not is irrelevant," one Latter-day Saint said. "Why? Because we believe in obeying the laws of the land."[43] "The United States could not long remain the great nation it is today if its citizens could refuse with impunity to obey the laws of the land," said a congressman, criticizing those who refused to be forcibly conscripted into war. "[Caesar's] law must have an authority supreme over the individual."[44] Churches should comply with IRS regulations because they "need to comply with the laws of the land," said one attorney.[45] George Sutherland, a justice on the US Supreme Court—and a Latter-day Saint—argued, in a ruling by the Court, that a person could not enjoy the benefits of citizenship without being willing to fight in potentially unjust wars. "Unqualified allegiance to the Nation and submission and obedience to the laws of the land . . . are not inconsistent with the will of God,"[46] he audaciously wrote.

But the law of the land is something different. As understood at the time of America's founding, and the era in which the aforementioned scriptures were recorded and the term used, the *law of the land* was not whatever Caesar said—it instead centered around the fundamental protection of one's God-given rights. Legal dictionaries all pointed to a definition given by Daniel Webster as a shared consensus about what it meant:

40. Marion G. Romney, "The Rule of Law," *Ensign*, February 1973.
41. Doctrine and Covenants 98:6.
42. Doctrine and Covenants 58:21.
43. "Obey The Laws Of The Land?," *Mormon Dialogue*, February 20, 2012, https://www.mormondialogue.org/topic/57002-obey-the-laws-of-the-land/.
44. Congressman Sam Gibbons, *Congressional Record: Proceedings and Debates of the 89th Congress, Second Session* (United States Government Printing Office, Washington, 1966), 347.
45. "Church Ministry Practice," Provident Law, accessed April 2, 2020, https://providentlawyers.com/practice-areas/church-ministry-practice/.
46. *United States v. Macintosh*, 283 U.S. 605 (1931).

> Perhaps no definition is more often quoted than that given by Mr. Webster in the Dartmouth College Case: "By the law of the land is most clearly intended the general law; a law which hears before it condemns; which proceeds upon inquiry, and renders judgment only after the trial. The meaning is that every citizen shall hold his life, liberty, property, and immunities, under the protection of the general rules which govern society. *Everything which may pass under the form of an enactment is not therefore to be considered the law of the land.*"[47]

General rules that govern society do not single out one group or favor certain people over another; they broadly protect the rights of each individual. And not every edict sent from Caesar is considered to be the law of the land, since these mandates often conflict with and violate those rights. What about the US Constitution, though? The document itself affirms that it is the "supreme law of the land," and we are supposed to "befriend" it. The scripture only refers to the "constitutional" law of the land which does not specify the United States Constitution per se. But constitutions can and do change, and plenty of them contain things that protect people in their life, liberty, and property. Consider the 1936 Constitution of the Union of Soviet Socialist Republics. Under section 10, titled "Fundamental Rights and Duties of Citizens," a long list of supposed rights are presented, including the right to "rest and leisure," "maintenance in old age and also in case of sickness or loss of capacity to work," and "education, including higher education, being free of charge." Rather than protecting existing rights, this document asserted entirely new ones that violate the rights of some to support others. Just because something is drafted or amended into a constitution does not mean it is valid, is supreme, or has divine backing.

The Lord clarified for us how someone who "keepeth the laws of God hath no need to break the laws of the land." In a preceding verse, He said: "For verily I say unto you, *my* law shall be kept on this land. Let no man think he is ruler; but let God rule him that judgeth."[48] God's law is harmonious with the law of the land; if we are obeying God, then there will be "no need to break the laws of the land" because we will be following them. But deviation from God's law—the imposition of Caesar's decrees—is not the law of the land. We are under no divine obligation to obey every random

47. Thomas M. Cooley, *A Treatise on the Constitutional Limitations Which Rest Upon the Legislative Power of the States of the American Union* (Boston: Little, Brown & Co., 1890), 431.
48. Doctrine and Covenants 58:19–20; emphasis added.

decree by another man who "think[s] he is ruler," particularly those decrees that violate our life, liberty, and property.

While it is true that God "suffered" the US Constitution to be established "by the hands of wise men whom [He] raised up unto this very purpose,"[49] God only *justified* our befriending of it. It is noteworthy that He did not command us to enthusiastically support it and reverence the document and the government it created, as so many today seem to do. To justify, in a theological sense, is "to pardon and clear from guilt; to absolve or acquit from guilt and merited punishment, and to accept as righteous on account of the merits of the Savior, or by the application of Christ's atonement to the offender."[50] In other words, by saying that we are justified in befriending the Constitution, it appears that God is merely saying it is okay that we do so—we are not guilty or wrong to do so. It is a fairly low standard, certainly not constituting divine praise. And it is not a commandment to proactively and eagerly champion the US Constitution. God did not want Israel to be ruled by kings, yet eventually consented to it—justified it, one might say—and even commanded Samuel to install a king,[51] despite the obstinate Israelites being warned about the oppressive implications of doing so. They wanted a Caesar like those of other nations, so He justified it.[52] Clearly God's justification and "establishment" of a system of law is not an endorsement that it is the divine ideal. We can and should do better.

And what of "this very purpose" for which God established the Constitution? It is, He said, because "it is not right that any man should be in bondage one to another."[53] The constitutional law of the land was (and is) ideally designed to broadly protect "the rights and protection of all flesh"[54]—and that is important for the Christian because our chief purposes are to worship God, spread the gospel, and exercise our agency in such a way that we follow God's commandments so as to one day return to His presence. That is our goal, and constraining Caesar to ensure we can remain focused on that task is ideally why the law of the land exists. But remember that Caesar's very existence—his nature, his motive, his satanic support system—encourages people to place one another in bondage. Dictatorships

---

49. Doctrine and Covenants 101:77–80.
50. "Justify," American Dictionary of the English Language, accessed June 20, 2020, http://webstersdictionary1828.com/Dictionary/justify.
51. 1 Samuel 8:19–22; 9:15–17.
52. This result was foreseen as described in Deuteronomy 17:14.
53. Doctrine and Covenants 101:79.
54. Doctrine and Covenants 101:77.

and democracies alike both involve subjecting one group of people to the whims of another.

Even the Pharisees were not so bold as to affirm that their man-made traditions, rules, and laws were "supreme." Yet Christians today tolerate, and often tout, a system in which Caesar's supremacy is affirmed. As one example, consider the controversy in which the restored Church of Jesus Christ found itself on the defense against a congressional inquiry over its religious practice involving plural marriages. Church leaders affirmed that polygamy was a right afforded to them under the First Amendment to the US Constitution, but this clause—prohibiting Congress from abridging the freedom of speech or prohibiting the free exercise of religion—was rendered impotent[55] by the majority that considered the practice repugnant.[56] The resulting 1879 US Supreme Court's decision in *Reynolds v. United States* argued the following, which was supported unanimously by all of the justices:

> Laws are made for the government of actions, and while they cannot interfere with mere religious belief and opinions, *they may with practices.* Suppose one believed that human sacrifices were a necessary part of religious worship, would it be seriously contended that the civil government under which he lived could not interfere to prevent a sacrifice? . . .
>
> So here, as a law of the organization of society under the exclusive dominion of the United States, it is provided that plural marriages shall not be allowed. Can a man excuse his practices to the contrary because of his religious belief? *To permit this would be to make the professed doctrines of religious belief superior to the law of the land.*[57]

Religious practice was shut down because allowing a group of people to express themselves (without harming others) in violation of Caesar's command was perceived as allowing God's law to be "superior to the law of the land." This ruling and its contention about Caesar's supremacy have become the legal basis to, among other things, punish a person for using peyote in a

---

55. The Morrill Anti-Bigamy Act was a federal law, signed by President Abraham Lincoln in 1862, which targeted the Mormon church by prohibiting polygamy and limiting church ownership of property. The subsequent Edmunds–Tucker Act, among many other provisions, disincorporated the church and directed the confiscation of church properties.

56. Mosiah 29:26 has King Mosiah arguing that his government should "do [its] business by the voice of the people," but this was a system of decentralized judges, who were merely interpreting and applying God's law that had been given to them (see verse 25).

57. *Reynolds v. United States*, 98 U.S. 145 (1878); emphasis added.

religious ceremony,[58] force a baker to create a celebratory cake in support of a marital practice he religiously opposes,[59] and coerce Catholics into providing birth control to their employees despite its conflict with their theological views.[60] Simply put, "religious practices in the United States are subject to federal, state, and local laws,"[61] and certainly, beyond strict religious practices, one's ability to freely use one's property, including money, without interference from the state. Despite the Supreme Being's thoughts on the matter, Caesar still considers himself supreme.

James Madison rightly recognized that the Constitution is a mere "parchment barrier" against "the encroaching spirit of power" that infects Caesars of all types.[62] While we are justified in befriending it, to the extent that it protects our rights and comports with God's law of the land, it should not be the object of our support. Christ should be.

The Twelfth Article of Faith

Many Christians are quick to point to Romans 13 as a defense for their position that we should submit to and support Caesar, but members of the restored Church of Jesus Christ instead will typically cite the twelfth article of faith. James E. Talmage, in his authoritative analysis (likewise titled *Articles of Faith*), argued bluntly that "it is the duty of the saints to submit themselves to the laws of their country."[63] Ezra Taft Benson characterized it as a "declaration requiring obedience, loyalty to, and respect for duly constituted laws and the officials administering those laws."[64] Church leaders have said that "members in any nation are obligated by the twelfth article

58. *Employment Division, Department of Human Resources of Oregon v. Smith*, 494 U.S. 872 (1990).
59. "In Narrow Decision, Supreme Court Sides With Baker Who Turned Away Gay Couple," *The New York Times*, June 4, 2018, https://www.nytimes.com/2018/06/04/us/politics/supreme-court-sides-with-baker-who-turned-away-gay-couple.html; the US Supreme Court ultimately, but very narrowly, ruled in the baker's favor.
60. "Dolan: White House 'Strangling' Catholic Church With Birth Control Mandate," CBS DC, May 22, 2012, https://washington.cbslocal.com/2012/05/22/dolan-white-house-strangling-catholic-church-with-birth-control-mandate/.
61. "Limits of Religious Freedom," *Harvard Political Review*, May 27, 2013, http://harvardpolitics.com/covers/limits-of-religious-freedom/.
62. James Madison, "No. XLVIII," *The Federalist* (Hallowell: Glazier, Masters & Smith, 1837), 234.
63. James E. Talmage, *Articles of Faith* (Salt Lake City: Deseret Book, 1984), 383.
64. Ezra Taft Benson, *God, Family, Country: Our Three Great Loyalties* (Salt Lake City: Bookcraft, 1974), 279.

of faith to obey the . . . laws of that nation."[65] From a young age, children are taught—using this article of faith—that "Heavenly Father wants us to be good citizens," which means "following the laws, or rules, of the places we live." And while governments are not perfect, "everyone can sustain, or strengthen and support, the government where they live."[66] Put more simply, children have been taught that our doctrinal belief is that "We believe in obeying the law."[67] Citing this Article, Russell M. Nelson said that Church leaders "encourage our members to be upright and loyal citizens in the countries that give them citizenship and to uphold governmental leaders and obey the civil laws wherever they live."[68]

Does the twelfth article of faith support and require these positions? Is it indeed our belief—and God's commandment—that we be "good citizens" and obey the law, period? Let's review what this statement of belief actually says: "We believe in being subject to kings, presidents, rulers, and magistrates, in obeying, honoring, and sustaining the law."[69]

Many read this statement, superficially, as suggesting absolute compliance to Caesar—an obligation to support him and do as asked. Part of the problem is the conventional understanding that has injected a coordinating conjunction into this statement—a connecting word that joins two separate, complete clauses into a longer sentence. For example, consider this sentence: "The traveler was tired, yet he continued walking to his destination." Each clause in this sentence is independent, but the coordinating conjunction "yet" combines them. With the twelfth article of faith, many church members seemingly believe it says "We believe in being subject to kings, presidents, rulers, and magistrates, *and* in obeying, honoring, and sustaining the law." This construction allows a person to infer that we believe in: 1) being subject to Caesar; and 2) obeying all his edicts. The person who adopts and advocates this misinterpretation therefore believes that we are obligated to simply do as we are told by whatever political organization claims authority to rule over us.

---

65. "Official policies and announcements," *Church News*, January 15, 1994, https://www.thechurchnews.com/archives/1994-01-15/official-policies-and-announcements-222-140843.
66. "Article of Faith 12," *Friend*, November 2015, https://www.churchofjesuschrist.org/study/friend/2015/11/article-of-faith-12.
67. "Lesson 31: I Will Obey the Law," *Primary 2: Choose the Right A* (1995), 162–67.
68. "Combatting Spiritual Drift—Our Global Pandemic," *Ensign*, November 1993, https://www.churchofjesuschrist.org/study/general-conference/1993/10/combatting-spiritual-drift-our-global-pandemic; this was from an address given at the 1993 Parliament of the World's Religions in Chicago, Illinois.
69. Articles of Faith 1:12.

But that is not what the statement says; there is no coordinating conjunction. The Article has one clause, not two. When read properly, the statement says that we believe in being subject to kings, presidents, rulers, and magistrates so long as—and to the extent that—*they* obey, honor, and sustain the law. Put differently, the description of adherence to law applies to Caesar, not to us. If Caesar follows the law, then we believe in being subject to him. If he does not, then we do not believe in being subject to him.

Therein lies a key conflict between Christ and Caesar, for "man's laws cannot make moral what God has declared immoral."[70] Christ calls on us to love others, without asterisks or exceptions. We are not to harm, defraud, or steal from others, whether directly or indirectly through intermediaries in government. Caesar's entire nature is to institutionalize the violation of these commandments and sanction them with flowery words—the greater good, general welfare, democracy, the will of the people, majority rule, representation, local control, and so on. Caesar's rhetoric is designed to assuage people's guilty consciences so they do not recognize that they are, in fact, guilty of violating God's law. Caesar calls evil good[71] and passes off as law things that God disapproves of. Meanwhile, many of God's children consider it His will that they—not just reluctantly, but earnestly—obey these mandates. But as explained earlier, the law that we all (including Caesar) must obey is more fundamental than the ever-changing whims of congressional majorities or despotic dictators, however benevolent or barbaric. We are only to follow other men—certainly Caesar, but even prophets and other ecclesiastical authorities—to the extent that they are following God.

Even assuming a generous interpretation in which the word *in* is indeed a continuation from one clause to the next, the twelfth article of faith is a mere summary statement meant to convey what is elsewhere in scripture. It was not a revelation from God, but rather part of a letter written by Joseph Smith to the editor of the *Chicago Democrat*, who had requested information about the nascent Latter-day Saint movement. Joseph provided a historical interview about the restoration of the gospel and then appended the letter with a concise summary of the key doctrines of the faith. As such, anyone who cites the twelfth article of faith to justify their views about broad submission to Caesar and his laws would have to support that view with a separate statement from God in support.

---

70. Dallin H. Oaks, "No Other Gods," *Ensign*, November 2013, https://www.churchofjesuschrist.org/study/general-conference/2013/10/no-other-gods.
71. Isaiah 5:20.

Doctrine and Covenants 134

While many use the twelfth article of faith to imply a divine obligation to submit to Caesar and comply with his decrees, a subsequent declaration of belief—also codified into scripture—adds important context to qualify the degree to which such compliance is justified. While Joseph Smith was away on missionary work, Oliver Cowdery read a document titled "Of Governments and Laws in General" to an assembly of church members. The assembly then approved the document for inclusion in a forthcoming publication of new scripture. The introductory statements make clear that this document was merely the opinion of church officers and not a revelation.[72] Nonetheless, it has been included in scripture and therefore some cite it in support of their views of Caesar.

Assuming, then, that this declaration of beliefs carries spiritual significance for Christians generally, what does it say and mean? One declaration asserts that a government's laws should be "framed and held inviolate as will secure to each individual the free exercise of conscience, the right and control of property, and the protection of life,"[73] effectively summarizing the "law of the land" principle discussed earlier. Other sections discuss the importance of justice, religious freedom, criminal consequences, and the rules of an orderly society. But the provision typically cited to support Caesar and his laws is this one:

> We believe that all men are bound to sustain and uphold the respective governments in which they reside, while protected in their inherent and inalienable rights by the laws of such governments; and that sedition and rebellion are unbecoming every citizen thus protected, and should be punished accordingly; and that all governments have a right to enact such laws as in their own judgments are best calculated to secure the public interest; at the same time, however, holding sacred the freedom of conscience.[74]

Many Latter-day Saints seemingly internalize only the first few words of this verse, leading them to incorrectly believe that God binds them to "sustain and uphold the [government] in which they reside," period. But again, the qualifying conditions that follow make clear that such allegiance is predicated on lawful activity. Our support is only required when we are

---

72. "Section 134, Earthly Governments and Laws," *Doctrine and Covenants Student Manual* (2002), 344–47.

73. Doctrine and Covenants 134:2.

74. Doctrine and Covenants 134:5.

"protected in [our] inherent and inalienable rights by the laws of such governments." Further, "sedition and rebellion are unbecoming every citizen *thus protected*."

A fair and plain reading of this declaration of belief results in the simple conclusion that when Caesar violates a person's rights, Caesar is not deserving of support. At a minimum, there is no divine obligation to simply submit to his many mandates. The very nature of the satanic state is that God's children are weaponized against one another, using Caesar's power to control and steal from other people. Government thus becomes "the great fiction through which everybody endeavors to live at the expense of everybody else,"[75] a continuation of the premortal war, with Lucifer still seeking to consolidate power and deceive the masses. "Governments must be righteous to receive the support of [Christians]," which includes "the full and unqualified right of the free exercise of individual liberty whenever it does not infringe upon the rights and liberties of others."[76] And while certain Caesars concede these points theoretically or codify them constitutionally, history clearly shows that "parchment barriers" do not prevent the violation of these rights. Caesar, by nature, attacks our liberty and entices us to do the same to one another.

As with the twelfth article of faith, anyone who cites the opinion expressed in these verses to justify their views about submission to Caesar has to support that view with a separate statement from God in agreement.

Civil Disobedience

After four months of imprisonment in a jail ironically named "Liberty," Joseph Smith, along with his Latter-day Saint followers, sought redress for the grievances to which they had been subjected. The Prophet departed Nauvoo for Washington, DC, accompanied by a few close friends "to lay before the Congress of the United States, the grievances of the Saints while in Missouri."[77] An initial meeting with President Martin Van Buren was followed up with a few months of lobbying senators and representatives in an unsuccessful attempt to find a champion for their cause. Finally, the

---

75. Frédéric Bastiat, *The Bastiat Collection*, vol. 1 (Auburn: Ludwig von Mises Institute, 2007), 99.
76. John A. Widtsoe, *Program of The Church of Jesus Christ of Latter-day Saints* (Salt Lake City: The Church of Jesus Christ of Latter-day Saints, 1937), 100.
77. B. H. Roberts, ed., *History of the Church of Jesus Christ of Latter-day Saints*, vol. 4 (Salt Lake City: Deseret Book, 1978), 19.

Prophet and his associates met with President Van Buren once more in February 1840, during which time he treated them rudely, according to Joseph, and told them: "Gentlemen, your cause is just, but I can do nothing for you . . . If I take up for you I shall lose the vote of Missouri."[78]

The systematic deprivation of the individual rights of the Saints—including, but not limited to, the rights to life, property, worship, and association—ultimately led Joseph to run for the office of President of the United States on an independent platform. Describing his reasons for pursuing the highest elected office in the nation, Joseph wrote:

> I would not have suffered my name to have been used by my friends on anywise as President of the United States, or candidate for that office, if I and my friends could have had the privilege of enjoying our religious and civil rights as American citizens, even those rights which the Constitution guarantees unto all her citizens alike. But this as a people we have been denied from the beginning. Persecution has rolled upon our heads from time to time, from portions of the United States, like peals of thunder, because of our religion; and no portion of the Government as yet has stepped forward for our relief. And in view of these things, I feel it to be my right and privilege to obtain what influence and power I can, lawfully, in the United States, for the protection of injured innocence.[79]

A contrasting distinction should be made at this point between civil disobedience as it is sometimes perceived—that is, the disobeying of a law with which one simply disagrees—and the rejection of a mandate unlawfully or unjustly imposed on others. Many Church leaders have been adamant in the past that Christians should not engage in civil disobedience. James E. Faust believed that we should "recognize the law of the land until it is changed."[80] Hugh B. Brown stated that the reasoning of those who advocate breaking the law "is fallacious and inconsistent with Christian principles."[81] And N. Eldon Tanner argued that "we adults can break no law with impunity without our children losing respect for the law."[82]

Despite these and other similar statements, however, there are numerous examples of justified and even praised civil disobedience in Church history. Helmuth Hübener, a German Latter-day Saint teenager, defied Hitler's

78. Ibid., 80.
79. Ibid., vol. 6, 210–11.
80. James E. Faust, "The Integrity of Obeying the Law," Freedom Festival Fireside, Provo, Utah, July 2, 1995.
81. In Conference Report, October 1965, 107–111.
82. In Conference Report, October 1964, 47.

propaganda machine by distributing leaflets containing news he picked up from the British Broadcasting Corporation using a shortwave radio. For these actions, he was eventually beheaded in a Gestapo prison. Latter-day Saints who know his story generally regard him as a heroic defender of freedom, despite his having broken Nazi law in carrying out his protests.

Another example is found in the actions of Alexander Doniphan, a Missouri lawyer, state representative, and member of the militia. Though not a member of their faith, Doniphan repeatedly defended the Saints against punitive legislation and government orders. When anti-Mormon troops surrounded Far West and ultimately forced its surrender, General Samuel D. Lucas ordered Doniphan to summarily execute Joseph Smith, along with six other leaders who were being held in custody. To this objectionable order, he responded: "It is cold-blooded murder. I will not obey your order . . . . If you execute these men I will hold you personally responsible before an earthly tribunal, so help me God."[83]

Scriptural examples of civil disobedience likewise abound, and a few are worth mentioning. When Pharaoh sent out a murderous decree that all male Israelite children be put to death, two Israelite midwives, Shiphrah and Puah, refused to comply. They protested that the Israelite women gave birth too quickly.[84] This allowed Moses's mother enough time to bend Pharaoh's order that all male Israelite babies be "cast into the river" by setting him afloat in a basket to preserve his life.[85] This man, Moses, whose life was the direct result of defiance to an unjust law, later opposed Pharaoh's government and freed his people from legalized bondage.[86]

David fled from Saul and evaded the troops sent by the king to slay him.[87] Daniel knowingly ignored the law that made praying to God illegal and "kneeled upon his knees three times a day, and prayed, and gave thanks before his God, as he did aforetime."[88] Shadrach, Meshach, and Abednego refused to obey the law that ordered them to worship idols in Babylon.[89] Peter and the other apostles were beaten and thrown in prison by the "authorities" who finally said, "Did we not straitly command you that

83. Roberts, History of the Church, vol. 3, 190–1.
84. Exodus 1: 16–19.
85. Exodus 1:22, 2:2.
86. Exodus 7–10.
87. Samuel 19.
88. Daniel 6:7–10.
89. Daniel 3:4–6, 12.

ye should not teach in [Christ's] name?" Peter's response: "We ought to obey God rather than men."[90]

This is a point that merits additional emphasis. *We ought to obey God rather than men.* Put differently, we should adhere to God's law of the land, and His divine principles of liberty and agency, rather than the conflicting dictates of Caesar, even when such dictates are popular with the majority. When John Taylor and other church leaders evaded the government's enforcement to end their practice of polygamy by hiding "on the underground" for years, it was because they, like Peter, considered it more important to obey God's law than man's. "What? Won't you submit to the dignity of the law?" Taylor rhetorically asked in an 1885 discourse.

> Well, I would if the law would only be a little dignified. But when we see the ermine bedraggled in the mud and mire, and every principle of justice violated, it behooves men to take care of themselves as best they may. That is what I have told people while I have been in the south—to take care of their liberties, to put their trust in the living God, to obey every constitutional law, and to adhere to all correct principles. But when men tamper with your rights and with your liberties . . . it is no longer a land of liberty, and it is certainly no longer a land of equal rights, and we must take care of ourselves as best we may, and avoid being caught in any of their snares . . . *Let us honor our God, and be true to those eternal principles which God has given us to hold sacred.* Keep them as sacredly as you would the apple of your eye. And while other men are seeking to trample the Constitution under foot, we will try to maintain it.[91]

When Caesar was violating the constitutional law of the land—the fundamental religious liberty and freedom of association—Taylor suggested resistance rather than submission. This was not defiance and disobedience, but the opposite; Caesar was wrong, and Taylor was trying to follow God.

Wilford Woodruff, Taylor's successor, carried on the same message. He had argued that the Saints were "ready to shoulder their guns and walk into these canyons and line them from here to Fort Bridger in defense of the Constitution of the United States and the rights which both the laws of God and man guarantee to us."[92]

Joseph F. Smith, decades later, still sang the same tune: "If lawmakers have a mind to . . . depart from the provisions of the Constitution where is the law human or divine, which binds me, as an individual, to outwardly

90. Acts 5:17–29; see Acts 4:17–21 for the original command.
91. John Taylor, *Journal of Discourses*, vol. 26 (Liverpool, 1886), 156.
92. Wilford Woodruff, *Journal of Discourses*, vol. 5 (Liverpool, 1858), 270.

and openly proclaim my acceptance of their acts?"[93] And stressing the earlier point, Smith argued that this resistance to unjust mandates was actually compliance with a higher law:

> Latter-day Saints . . . are the most law-abiding, the most peaceable, long-suffering and patient people that can today be found within the confines of this republic, and perhaps anywhere else upon the face of the earth; and we intend to continue to be law-abiding so far as the constitutional law of the land is concerned.[94]

John Taylor also said,

> If it be treason to stand up for our Constitutional rights . . . if it be treason to resist the unconstitutional acts of a vitiated and corrupt administration . . . if it be treason to maintain inviolate the Constitution and institutions of the United States, when nearly all the states are seeking to trample them under their feet—then indeed are we guilty of treason.[95]

But it is not treason. Christian civil disobedience is not merely a flippant refusal to do what you are told, but rather a faith-based effort to fulfill God's law. It is a rejection of Caesar's pretended authority and a submission to the source of true authority. It is not disobedience, then, but *obedience* to law that leads the earnest Christian to refuse compliance to Caesar and the mandates he wrongly claims are valid law. However, resisting Caesar is more often about refusing to participate in his systems and spoils than it is having to confront a direct command that contradicts God's will. Christians rarely experience a mandate from the state that requires them to go against their faith. More often, they are seduced into using its power, processes, and benefits to enrich themselves at the expense of others and control the behavior of their neighbors. We might like to consider ourselves cut from the same cloth as Peter or Shadrach, Meshach, and Abednego, ready to resist the government when it aims to stop us from doing what God explicitly has said we ought to. But it is in small things[96] that our true loyalty is made manifest—decisions such as whether to support raising taxes on others, regulating their use of property, preventing them from ingesting something, and so forth. Caesar provides us many ways to go against Christ, most of them minor and "part of the process."

93. Joseph F. Smith, *Journal of Discourses*, vol. 23 (Liverpool, 1883), 71.
94. Ibid.
95. John Taylor, *The Latter-day Saints' Millennial Star*, vol. 45 (Liverpool, 1883), 168.
96. Alma 37:6; Doctrine and Covenants 123:16.

For situations that do result in overt conflict between Christ and Caesar, it is one thing to discuss whether we are divinely obligated to obey the latter's laws. It is another thing to determine whether we should disobey them. Most reluctantly and strategically submit to something in order to avoid the consequences of not doing so. Just as a child begrudgingly does his chores in order to avoid being disciplined, those over whom Caesar wields power may comply with his edicts merely to avoid provoking his ire so that they can carry on with their desired activities. When circumstances change and it becomes necessary or important to resist, there are important decisions to be made. Traditional (and non-violent) civil disobedience typically entails a public defiance of an unjust law along with suffering the imposed consequences as an educational act to help others see the wrongness of the situation. "Every revolution begins with a single act of defiance," as the saying goes—a refrain demonstrated by colonists revolting against the most powerful country in the world. These colonists were led by men who God had "raised up unto this very purpose."[97] The severity of the consequence, and the degree of injustice created by the law being challenged, helps inform us in determining whether to defy Caesar. It may not be prudent to risk years or a lifetime of incarceration for refusing to pay an unjust tax, for example, especially as this would detract from our purpose in life: our ability to raise a family, serve others, spread the gospel, and so on. As the Declaration of Independence notes, "mankind is more disposed to suffer—while evils are sufferable—than to right themselves by abolishing the forms to which they are accustomed." If a Christian can reasonably tolerate Caesar's mandates so as to preserve the (albeit limited) freedom and capacity to pursue their divine obligations, then that is likely the prudent course of action.

A Christian does not defy Caesar for the sake of doing so. After all, "whosoever shall compel thee to go a mile, go with him twain."[98] The purpose is not resistance per se, but rather compliance; a Christian is simply trying to focus on and follow God's commandments. Defying any conflicting mortal mandates is merely a by-product of following the Way. While Caesar tempts us to take any number of detours, a Christian following the Way is not disregarding alternative routes so much as choosing to pursue the correct path. Rejection of Caesar is a side effect of following Christ.

97. Doctrine and Covenants 101:80.
98. Matthew 5:42.

Summary

We did not come to Earth excited to be controlled by our peers. This period of our life, our mortal probation, is a continuation of the competition for our loyalty and worship—the divine duel between Christ and Lucifer, and his Caesarean subordinates. Our task continues to be what it was before: to choose God over any counterfeit and pursue the steps necessary to return to Him. There are many who demand our loyalty and desire our worship; the temptation to want to rule over others is quite strong, and satanic.[99] It is the "nature and disposition of almost all men, as soon as they get a little authority, *as they suppose*, they will immediately begin to exercise unrighteous dominion."[100] Caesar eagerly provides a mechanism through which this control can be exerted, but in the process, God's "law of the land" is undermined and the agency of each person attacked.

Those who "suppose" they have authority over others have long been eager to persuade Christians that "even a tyrant enjoyed divinely ordained authority and was owed the same loyalty and obedience as a good prince."[101] And once he has reached a critical mass, Caesar can sit back and let the supportive subjects preach it to their peers. Colonists loyal to the Crown cheered on the many clergy who preached submission and argued against revolution, for "if even the most vile tyrants like Nero deserved obedience, how could it be just to resist George III?"[102] In the words of a pastor in Boston, "disobedience to civil rulers in the due exercise of their authority is not merely a political sin, but a heinous offense against God."[103]

In a later era, featuring fierce debate over the morality and legality of slavery, ministers cited the Bible in support of the practice. Making matters worse, the federal government passed the Fugitive Slave Act, which legally compelled individuals to help return escaped slaves to their former masters. The *Richmond Daily Dispatch*, channeling the cultural zeitgeist, claimed that "hundreds" of "passages from Scripture [prove that] slavery has the divine sanction,"[104]

---

99. Moses 6:15; Helaman 7:5; 2 Nephi 5:3.
100. Doctrine and Covenants 121:39; emphasis added.
101. Monica Stensland, *Habsburg Communication in the Dutch Revolt* (Amsterdam: Amsterdam University Press, 2012) 106.
102. William Anthony Hay, "The Loyalist Arguments," The Russell Kirk Center, June 30, 2019, https://kirkcenter.org/reviews/the-loyalist-arguments/.
103. Jonathan Mayhew, *A Discourse Concerning Unlimited Submission and Non-Resistance to the Higher Powers* (Boston: D. Fowle, 1750), 10.
104. *The Daily Dispatch*, July 6 1855, https://chroniclingamerica.loc.gov/lccn/sn84024738/1855-07-06/ed-1/seq-2/.

including Romans 13, which allegedly demanded people help return fugitive slaves. A North Carolina paper complained against "these Christians in the free States [who] set up their judgments against that of the Almighty, and blindly strike against all law, order, and right!"[105] As Hitler rose to power, many pastors preached from Romans 13 in churches adorned with Nazi banners and flags, reminding worshippers about their obligation to obey authority.[106]

More recently, this misinterpreted biblical passage was cited in defense of the federal government's forceful separation of parents and children crossing into America's southern border. Some parents were not even told that their children were being taken. In one case, Border Patrol agents told a mother they were taking her daughter to be bathed, but they never returned the girl.[107] The US Attorney General, Jeff Sessions, defended the policy separating children: "I would cite you to the Apostle Paul and his clear and wise command in Romans 13, to obey the laws of the government because God has ordained them for the purpose of order," he insufferably said. "Orderly and lawful processes are good in themselves and protect the weak and lawful." The press secretary, whose father, former governor Mike Huckabee, was a pastor, doubled down on the same idea: "It is very biblical to enforce the law."[108]

Caesar benefits from the confusion among Christians pertaining to how, when, or whether they must submit to and support the state. "Satan doth stir up the hearts of the people to contention," the Lord says, "concerning the points of my doctrine; and in these things they do err, for they do wrest the scriptures and do not understand them."[109] Some of this confusion was intentional, in order to "blind the eyes and harden the hearts of the children of men."[110] As a result, God's children fail to understand "the things which are prepared for them"[111] if only they choose Christ over any counterfeit Caesar.

---

105. *North Carolina Standard*, October 30, 1850, https://chroniclingamerica.loc.gov/lccn/sn84045030/1850-10-30/ed-1/seq-2/.
106. "The Fight to Define Romans 13," *The Atlantic*, June 15, 2018, https://www.theatlantic.com/ideas/archive/2018/06/romans-13/562916/.
107. "Civil & Human Rights Groups File Emergency Request to Inter-American Commission on Human Rights to Stop Family Separations, Reunite Families," Texas Civil Rights Project, May 31, 2018, https://texascivilrightsproject.org/civil-rights-groups-family-separations/.
108. "Why is Jeff Sessions quoting Romans 13 and why is the bible verse so often invoked?," *USA Today*, June 16, 2018, https://www.usatoday.com/story/news/2018/06/16/jeff-sessions-bible-romans-13-trump-immigration-policy/707749002/.
109. Doctrine and Covenants 10:63; Moses 4:4.
110. 1 Nephi 13:27; 12:17.
111. Doctrine and Covenants 78:10.

THE BOOK OF MORMON

In early 2017, twenty-four-year-old Amber VanHecke embarked on a solo journey from her home state of Texas to the Grand Canyon, relying on the Google Maps app to guide her the entire way. Isolated in the Arizona desert, she took notice of her car's fuel indicator, which said she had enough to travel an additional seventy miles. The map reassured her that she was only thirty-five miles away from a highway, where she assumed she would encounter a gas station nearby. Amber trusted the technology, which instructed her to turn onto a road that did not actually exist. But she continued on, assuming that the information was correct—and then she ran out of gas and was stranded alone in the middle of the desert. Amber formed a large "HELP" distress sign out of nearby rocks and built signal fires, hoping to catch the attention of planes passing overhead. Five days later, she still had no luck. "It was just cries of despair," she said. "I was sobbing, and I was very scared. I felt like maybe this is where I die."[1] Having survived to that point on the meager supply of water and snacks she had, she hiked 11 miles through the desert until her phone caught enough of a signal for her to dial 911 and get the help she desperately needed.

Bad information has led to similarly disastrous results in many other situations. When it is accidental, it is unfortunate—as in the case of a woman who came home to find her home destroyed after Google Maps provided the

1. "Denton woman to recount ordeal stranded in Arizona desert on ABC's '20/20'," *The Dallas Morning News*, March 31, 2017, https://www.dallasnews.com/news/2017/03/31/denton-woman-to-recount-ordeal-stranded-in-arizona-desert-on-abc-s-20-20/.

demolition crew with the wrong location,[2] or in the case of three Washington women who drove into a lake in the dark of night, submerging their vehicle, after the GPS directed them to turn onto a road that was actually a boat launch.[3] But misinformation is often malicious, with people preying on the ignorant who are duped into acting in ways that they otherwise would not. From fraudulent financial scams to political campaigns bending the truth, people are often controlled—in most cases, unwittingly—by other people pulling the strings. As the master propagandist Edward Bernays once wrote:

> Those who manipulate the organized habits and opinions of the masses constitute an invisible government which is the true ruling power of the country . . . . It remains a fact that in almost every act of our daily lives, whether in the sphere of politics or business, in our social conduct or our ethical thinking, we are dominated by a relatively small number of persons . . . . It is they who pull the wires which control the public mind, who harness old social forces and contrive new ways to bind and guide the world.[4]

With so many Christians supporting Caesar, one must ask: has Jesus's message been watered down or lost? If Caesar can weaponize passages like Romans 13 against Christians, with so many disciples of Jesus failing to reject His counterfeit, then has the Bible fallen short as an instrument to teach God's word and warn followers how to avoid forbidden detours and distractions? Because of the "confusion and strife among the different denominations"[5] of Christianity, "division is multiplied, uncertainty increases, and humanity [is] distracted with the cries of discordant sects contending over their creed."[6] Christ "is not the author of confusion,"[7] yet Christians are clearly confused. From the earliest days in His church, disciples were warned that "grievous wolves [would] enter in among [them]," suggesting external threats, and that internal issues would also be prevalent: "also of your own selves shall men arise, speaking perverse things, to draw away disciples after them."[8] False prophets[9] would lead many to "turn

---

2. "Woman's home demolished after Google Maps error," CNN, March 25, 2016, https://money.cnn.com/2016/03/25/technology/google-maps-house/.
3. "GPS leads lost driver down boat ramp," KVAL 13, June 15, 2011, https://kval.com/news/offbeat/gps-leads-lost-driver-down-boat-ramp.
4. Edward Bernays, *Propaganda* (Brooklyn: Ig Publishing, 2005), 9, 19.
5. Joseph Smith—History 1:8.
6. *The Latter-day Saints' Millennial Star*, vol. XLIX (Liverpool: George Teasdale, 1887), 72.
7. 1 Corinthians 14:33.
8. Acts 20:29–30.
9. Matthew 24:24.

away their ears from the truth."[10] Original teachings of Christ and His apostles were written and circulated "in purity,"[11] but the "plain and most precious" portions were "taken away"[12] due to "ignorant translators, careless transcribers, or designing and corrupt priests [who] committed many errors,"[13] "perverting the right ways of the Lord, that they might blind the eyes and harden the hearts of the children of men."[14] These doctrinal distortions in what eventually became the Bible have caused "an exceedingly great many [to] stumble,"[15] allowing Satan to gain "great power"[16] as a result. The whore thrives when Christians are confused and do not follow the Way.

But God did not want His children to "forever remain in that awful state of blindness,"[17] and therefore planned to bring forth "much of [His] gospel, which [is] plain and precious."[18] That additional record of scripture is now known as the Book of Mormon, named after its editor who compiled a series of ancient records documenting the history of a branch of the children of Israel who departed Jerusalem several centuries before Christ's birth. The "central purpose of the Book of Mormon is its testament of Jesus Christ." This is especially evident in the fact that of the "more than 6,000 verses . . . far more than half refer directly to Him."[19] Where the Bible has caused some doctrinal confusion due to differing interpretations, this second scriptural witness provides much needed clarity.

That clarity is particularly important when it comes to how Christians ought to act regarding Caesar; this testament of Jesus Christ is replete with warnings that need to be heeded if one is to follow God fully—warnings that many members of the restored Church of Jesus Christ fail to heed. The added scripture was given to us not merely to better learn about Jesus and feel spiritually enlightened, but that we might "know how to combat false educational, political, religious, and philosophical concepts."[20] It is a

10. 2 Timothy 4:3–4.
11. 1 Nephi 13:25.
12. 1 Nephi 13:26.
13. Joseph Smith, *The Latter-day Saints' Millennial Star*, vol. XXII (Liverpool: Amasa Lyman, 1860), 263.
14. 1 Nephi 13:27.
15. 1 Nephi 13:29.
16. 1 Nephi 13:24.
17. 1 Nephi 13:32.
18. 1 Nephi 13:34.
19. Boyd K. Packer, "The Book of Mormon: Another Testament of Jesus Christ—Plain and Precious Things," *Ensign*, May 2005; see also 2 Nephi 25:26.
20. Ezra Taft Benson, *The Teachings of Ezra Taft Benson* (Salt Lake City: Bookcraft, 1988), 56.

warning manual as much as a inspiring theological text. If we fail to heed the warning, we have not used it to its fullest purpose. And while "the Book of Mormon narrative is a chronicle of nations long since gone," like good scripture ought to, it contains "descriptions of the problems of today's society [that are] as current as the morning newspaper and much more definitive, inspired, and inspiring concerning the solutions of those problems,"[21] including people who "succumbed to the wiles of ambitious and scheming leaders who oppressed them with burdensome taxes . . . [and] led the people into terrible wars that resulted in the death of millions and the final and total extinction of two great civilizations in two different eras."[22] Caesar is as Caesar does. This book of scripture, quite unlike the Bible, warns its readers "plainly that ye cannot err"[23] in order to help us avoid a similar fate.

A Forgotten Focal Point

The pinnacle passage in the Book of Mormon is the visitation of Jesus Christ to His followers on the American continent after his resurrection,[24] an event He foretold during his ministry in Jerusalem.[25] This visit was a culmination of centuries of prophecy by Christ's disciples in the Americas who testified of His coming, abided by his teachings, and encouraged their fellow men to repent and prepare for that glorious day. It makes sense that this passage receives so much attention from those who read the book.

But for all its importance and well-deserved attention, there is another focal point in the Book of Mormon that is often overlooked, but critical to understanding why Christ and Caesar cannot be reconciled. Whereas the teachings of and prophecies about Christ permeate the scriptural record and come into focus in 3 Nephi, Chapter 11, the warnings about satanic "secret combinations" likewise litter the Book of Mormon and come into focus in Ether, Chapter 8. This secondary emphasis recorded by the book's authors is no less significant and is equally applicable to our day. Our collective failure to understand and respond to the warnings it contains makes us extremely susceptible to the same result recorded by Mormon: the spiritual

---

21. Gordon B. Hinckley, "An Angel from on High, the Long, Long Silence Broke," *Ensign*, November 1979.
22. Ibid.
23. Alma 5:43.
24. 3 Nephi 11.
25. John 10:16.

degradation and eventual destruction of our entire society. It is a warning about why Caesar and his tactics must be understood and rejected.

Known at times as the Gadianton Robbers, the Book of Mormon's chief antagonists rose to such power that they were able to overtake the Nephite government[26] and oppress God's people through the power of the state. Their nefarious deeds,[27] including predatory flattery, deception, infiltration, murder, plunder, and "whoredoms and all manner of wickedness, contrary to the laws of their country and also the laws of their God" led the prophet Mormon to note that the group "did prove the overthrow, yea, almost the entire destruction of the people of Nephi."[28] The alarming rise in wickedness among the Nephites[29] and their direct support of and participation in secret combinations[30] proved to be their ultimate downfall, as predicted by many previous prophecies.[31]

When Mormon's son, Moroni, compiled the book of Ether to summarize what had happened to the earlier Jaredite civilization, he likewise attributed its downfall and ultimate destruction[32] to a Gadianton-esque group of conspiring criminals who were able "to gain power, and to murder, and to plunder, and to lie, and to commit all manner of wickedness and whoredoms."[33] With two examples of similar circumstances, a pattern began to emerge. As the final caretaker over the records, Moroni was able to review past writings and observe historical trends spanning more than a millennium. Taking that long view of history, he recognized and emphatically stated that evil forces conspired to successfully dismantle the moral and functional underpinnings of the two societies. With that observation in mind, he proceeded to offer counsel directly to latter-day readers of the book and convey a commandment from God:

> Wherefore, O ye Gentiles, it is wisdom in God that these things should be shown unto you, that thereby ye may repent of your sins, and suffer not that these murderous combinations shall get above you, which are built up to get power and gain—and the work, yea, even the work of destruction come upon you, yea, even the sword of the justice of the

26. Helaman 6:39.
27. Helaman 6:23.
28. Helaman 2:13.
29. Helaman 6:31.
30. Helaman 6:38.
31. 1 Nephi 12:14–19; 2 Nephi 26:10; Jacob 3:3; Enos 1:13; Alma 9:18–24; Alma 45:10–14; Helaman 7:17–23; Helaman 15.
32. Ether 8:21.
33. Ether 8:16.

> Eternal God shall fall upon you, to your overthrow and destruction if ye shall suffer these things to be.
>
> Wherefore, the Lord commandeth you, when ye shall see these things come among you that ye shall awake to a sense of your awful situation, because of this secret combination which shall be among you; or wo be unto it, because of the blood of them who have been slain; for they cry from the dust for vengeance upon it, and also upon those who built it up.
>
> For it cometh to pass that whoso buildeth it up seeketh to overthrow the freedom of all lands, nations, and countries; and it bringeth to pass the destruction of all people, for it is built up by the devil, who is the father of all lies; even that same liar who beguiled our first parents, yea, even that same liar who hath caused man to commit murder from the beginning; who hath hardened the hearts of men that they have murdered the prophets, and stoned them, and cast them out from the beginning.
>
> Wherefore, I, Moroni, am commanded to write these things that evil may be done away, and that the time may come that Satan may have no power upon the hearts of the children of men, but that they may be persuaded to do good continually, that they may come unto the fountain of all righteousness and be saved.[34]

These conspiring forces are "built up by the devil" to "get power and gain" and to "overthrow [our] freedom"—the very essence of Caesar and the motive of those seduced by his statist systems that allow individuals to exert control over their neighbors and be enriched at their expense. We are told that the same abominable elements that felled two previous civilizations are likewise operating in our own day, working towards the same ends as before. We are also told that God has commanded us to recognize these influences—the first step in counteracting their effects and rejecting affiliation with them. And we are given context regarding the eternal struggle this rolls into; these are not just some independently-operating wicked men lusting for power. Rather, Satan is marshaling his forces to oppose God's kingdom just as he always has.

The Book of Mormon contains a lengthy list of passages detailing the degree to which Satan and his minions have worked to oppose and oppress God's followers. Throughout the book, we read of prophecies and warnings when God's people were repeatedly told that if they succumbed to or supported such secret combinations, they would be destroyed. Finally, we see how that prophecy was fulfilled, and are directly told that the same situation applies to us. For this reason, Moroni's warning serves as a second focal

34. Ether 8:23–26.

point in the Book of Mormon. While the book teaches of Christ, it likewise teaches about His antithesis. While we are invited to follow Jesus, we are also invited to reject the enemy. And while 3 Nephi 11 describes the glory of Christ's visit, Ether 8 warns us to steer clear of its opposite. We ignore the latter chapter at our peril.

Failing to recognize this additional emphasis of the Book of Mormon, which is almost entirely absent from the Bible,[35] sets up Latter-day Saints for confusion, and thus unwitting collusion with Caesar. For example, most Book of Mormon readers seem to believe that secret combinations are gangs, the mafia, Islamic terrorists, or other such troublemakers. These uninformed views completely avoid the clear picture painted by scripture,[36] which shows that the most basic benchmark, other than the obvious lust for power and riches, is that they overtake control of the government. This is achieved not by violent revolution or external attacks, but by internal infestation. It was precisely because these combinations were able to "obtain the sole management of the government"[37] that they were successful in their broader efforts to undermine the Christian cause. The goal pursued by Satan's helpers is that of "filling the judgment-seats" of government in order to "[usurp] the power and authority of the land."[38] With this criteria in place, it becomes evident that gang members or terrorists are not who qualifies as a secret combination, and it is also easy to see how such forces can undermine an entire society. Those involved in secret combinations of this sort are far more difficult for people to label, for unlike mafia members and cave-dwelling terrorists, those guilty of these offenses look like us. They speak the same language, wear the same attire, and, like the wolf in sheep's clothing, mask themselves so well that they remain largely undetected.[39] Satan "is working under such perfect disguise that many do not recognize either him or his methods."[40] Those who read the Book of Mormon but do not recognize

35. A couple exceptions might include Ezekiel 22:23–30 and Jeremiah 11:8–10.

36. Unfortunately, there have been institutional reasons contributing to the ignorance. The long-used Gospel Doctrine manual for the Book of Mormon relegated Ether 8 to the "additional teaching ideas" at the bottom of the weekly lesson, not covering the topic of secret combinations at all in the main lesson content, despite Moroni's explicit and emphatic warning.

37. Helaman 6:39.

38. Helaman 7:4.

39. Helaman 1:12.

40. In James R. Clark, comp., *Messages of the First Presidency of The Church of Jesus Christ of Latter-day Saints*, vol. 6 (1965–75), 179.

Satan's disguises cannot heed its warnings that would help them identify and reject such methods. Even the elect will be deceived.[41]

In his day, Mormon observed that "notwithstanding the great destruction which hung over my people, they did not repent of their evil doings."[42] Instead, God's people aligned with the adversary's forces and chose to "build them up and support them."[43] Aiming to stave off a repetition in the latter days, he and his son Moroni warned us to learn from the mistakes they documented and "suffer not that these murderous combinations shall get above you."[44] Many Christians, being seduced by Caesar, similarly build up and support secret combinations that are working towards the same goals that the scriptures prove have long been pursued.

The Book of Mormon is another testament of Jesus Christ. We rightly tell the world that this book contains potent and prophetic teachings about who Christ is and how one ought to act on that information. But this summary of the book is woefully inadequate if we sideline the secondary message: stay away from Caesar's secret combinations, or suffer the same fate as the societies whose destruction the book documents.

Abuse of Power

While the Book of Mormon does contain explicit warnings about the more sinister elements of the state—secret combinations—it also has profound insights and warnings about the more elementary aspects of Caesar, such as taxation, oppression of others, and authority. One such Book of Mormon narrative is also described in the Bible: the propensity of people to exploit power for their benefit at others' expense. Just as Samuel warned the children of Israel that embracing secular rule (in their case, through a king) would result in heavy taxation and pseudo-enslavement,[45] the Nephite record is replete with similar examples, documenting the downsides of Caesarean power structures.

The earliest chronological example comes from the nascent Jaredite nation, an offshoot from the time when the Tower of Babel was built.[46] Jared, his brother, and their families traveled along with a few other families

41. Joseph Smith—Matthew 1:22.
42. Mormon 2:8.
43. Helaman 6:38.
44. Ether 8:23.
45. 1 Samuel 8:10–18.
46. Ether 1:33; Omni 1:22.

to a new land prepared for them by God. Then, in their old age, Jared and his brother gathered their posterity to see if the now numerous people had any last requests before the brothers died. Predictably, "the people desired of them that they should anoint one of their sons to be a king over them." Jared's brother, considering the request "grievous," echoed Samuel, thus confirming a divine witness[47] to the truth: "Surely this thing leadeth to captivity."[48] The book of Ether offers ample evidence to prove this prophecy came true with literal bloodshed occurring as a result of kingly domination. But the issue was bigger than a mere monarchy—this form of government was a rejection of God and a centralization of power that competing parties sought to wrest control of. The Caesarean temptation to seek for power and wealth[49] at others' expense ultimately caused the downfall of an entire nation because they abandoned Christ as their focus.

The Nephite nation was no less immune to the desire for kingly control and subsequent rejection[50] of God as their ruler. Nephi himself records that his people, centuries after Jared's, "would that I should be their king"—a proposal he rejected, since he "was desirous that they should have *no* king."[51] But this did not last long, as Nephi himself ultimately "anointed a man to be a king and a ruler over his people" just before his death.[52] In general, the Nephite kings were righteous and served a dual role as religious ministers to the people, thus more closely resembling a theocracy than a monarchy. For hundreds of years, they maintained this system of government until King Mosiah obtained and translated the Jaredite record,[53] which revealed the inherent dangers that come with centralized power and rulers that compete with Christ for glory, worship, and power. It was immediately after this infusion of knowledge[54] that Mosiah asked his people to reconsider[55] their desire for a king. No doubt with the bloody Jaredite battles on his mind, he told them "I fear there would rise contentions among you . . . which would be the cause of shedding much blood and perverting the way of the Lord, yea, and destroy the souls of many people."[56] With ample evidence from his translation

47. 2 Corinthians 13:1.
48. Ether 6:21–23; 7:5.
49. Ether 9:11.
50. 1 Samuel 8:7.
51. 2 Nephi 5:18; emphasis added.
52. Jacob 1:9.
53. Mosiah 28:17.
54. Mosiah 28:18.
55. Mosiah 29:5.
56. Mosiah 29:7.

effort, he exclaimed "how much iniquity doth one wicked king cause to be committed, yea, and what great destruction!"[57] And to reinforce the historical record, he reminded his people of the recently deposed King Noah, whose "wickedness and abominations" lead to "great destruction" and bondage.[58]

Beyond practical concerns about abusive leadership from wicked kings, Mosiah homed in on a principle that undermines Caesar's entire claim to power. He told them, "because all men are not just it is not expedient that ye should have a king or kings to rule over you."[59] Because of man's fallible nature, Mosiah rightly calls into question the system of mortals ruling over one another—something that dictators, presidents, governors, mayors, and kings all share to varying degrees. Positions of power attract "king-men,"[60] who desire to control others. It is an unfortunate truism that "when the wicked rule, the people mourn."[61] It is "precisely because some people are evil and because they tend to dominate the good that the state should be abolished."[62] And so, King Mosiah wisely pushed for a different path, to "do that which will make for the peace of this people,"[63] by introducing a decentralized system of judges, who would interpret and apply God's law. The king's about-face, inspired by lessons learned from the Jaredite nation and King Noah's reign, deserves to be quoted at length:

> And I command you to do these things [selecting judges] in the fear of the Lord; and I command you to do these things, and that ye have no king; that if these people commit sins and iniquities they shall be answered upon their own heads.
>
> For behold I say unto you, the sins of many people have been caused by the iniquities of their kings; therefore their iniquities are answered upon the heads of their kings.
>
> And now I desire that this inequality should be no more in this land, especially among this my people; but I desire that this land be a land of liberty, and every man may enjoy his rights and privileges alike . . .

57. Mosiah 29:17.
58. Mosiah 29:18.
59. Mosiah 29:16.
60. Alma 51:5–8.
61. Doctrine and Covenants 98:9.
62. Alexandre Christoyannopoulos, *Christian Anarchism: A Political Commentary on the Gospel* (Exeter: Imprint Academic, 2011), 183.
63. Mosiah 29:10.

> And he also unfolded unto them all the disadvantages they labored under, by having an unrighteous king to rule over them;
>
> Yea, all his iniquities and abominations, and all the wars, and contentions, and bloodshed, and the stealing, and the plundering, and the committing of whoredoms, and all manner of iniquities which cannot be enumerated—telling them that these things ought not to be, that they were expressly repugnant to the commandments of God.[64]

It cannot get clearer than that: a God-fearing king recognized that substituting mortal rulers for God is "expressly repugnant" to God's will. Such systems of power cause contention, including stealing and plundering, which are the essence of Caesar's operations, empowering people to live at the expense of others. Mosiah instead told his people to reject this "inequality," which inhibited people from enjoying their rights. The people, in turn, were "convinced of the truth of his words" and "relinquished their desires for a king."[65]

A superficial takeaway from this section of scripture would be that self-rule is superior to top-down governance, and therefore systems of government such as a constitutional republic with voter representation are sufficient, if not ideal. But the Book of Mormon says otherwise; what was before a relatively peaceful existence under Nephite monarchy devolved into a story of turbulence and violence. From the time that Mosiah instituted the "reign of the judges" until Christ's post-resurrection arrival, there are fifteen major war campaigns recorded. Most readers seem to believe that the war-soaked pages of the book of Alma feature an us-versus-them campaign, wherein wicked Lamanites constantly fight the righteous Nephites. A quote attributed to Cicero explains the hidden reality of the Nephite nation during this self-governing period:

> A nation can survive its fools, and even the ambitious. But it cannot survive treason from within. An enemy at the gates is less formidable, for he is known and carries his banner openly. But the traitor moves amongst those within the gate freely, his sly whispers rustling through all the alleys, heard in the very halls of government itself.
>
> For the traitor appears not a traitor; he speaks in accents familiar to his victims, and he wears their face and their arguments, he appeals to the baseness that lies deep in the hearts of all men. He rots the soul of a nation, he works secretly and unknown in the night to undermine the pillars of the city, he infects the body politic so that it can no longer resist. A murderer is less to fear.

---

64. Mosiah 29:30–32, 35–36.
65. Mosiah 29:37–38.

A common thread among *all fifteen* of these wars is that they were instigated by dissenting Nephites who aspired for power, broke away from the group and through various means incited the Lamanites to riot and war against the Nephites. In light of this pattern, it becomes clear that the Lamanites had largely become pawns in a war of propaganda, corralled and controlled by power-seeking authoritarians. The fifteen provocations are:

1.	Amlici	Alma 2
2.	The People of Ammonihah	Alma 8:3, 9, 16; 10:27–32; 16:1–11; 25:1–8; 49:3
3.	Amalekites	Alma 21:3–6; 23:7–14; 24; 27:1–3
4.	Zoramites	Alma 31:8; 43:3–17
5.	Amalickiah	Alma 46–49; 51:9–12, 22–37
6.	Morianton	Alma 50:25–35
7.	King-Men	Alma 51:8; 15–21; 60:14–18
8.	Ammoron	Alma 52:19–20; 33–36; 59:7; 62:33–36
9.	Pachus	Alma 61:3–20; 62:1–11
10.	Nephite Dissenters	Alma 63:10–15
11.	Coriantumr and Tubaloth	Helaman 1
12.	Prideful Nephites	Helaman 4
13.	Gadianton Robbers	Helaman 10:18–19; 11:1–10
14.	Dissenters and Gadianton Robbers	Helaman 11:21–26
15.	Giddianhi	3 Nephi 1:27; 2–4

If the descriptions of these events truly are "as current as the morning newspaper,"[66] then it follows that these details, and their implications about political power, deserve heightened attention. Mormon's inclusion of these wars implies that our threats are no different than those his country

66. Hinckley, "An Angel from on High, the Long, Long Silence Broke."

faced. He and his son tell us in no uncertain terms that the conspirators, tied together with their common philosophy, caused the destruction of two entire societies, and issue a clarion call at the end of their record nearly begging us to pay attention and learn from past mistakes.

The Book of Mormon tells us in plain language and through repeated examples that our biggest threats are amongst us, rather than in distant lands. "Ye hear of wars in far countries," the Lord says, "and you say that there will soon be great wars in far countries, but ye know not the hearts of men in your own land."[67] It is easy to believe that the evil Lamanites were the Nephites' real problem, and thereby infer that today's threats are similarly external, but this requires mental gymnastics that the scriptures do not support. Instead, "there are within the very borders of [our own country] those who . . . would force upon us the same type of government that Lucifer advocates in the councils of heaven."[68] Satan can do from within that which he cannot do from without. This is how secret combinations operated in the Jaredite and Nephite nations, and it is precisely because of political power and Caesarean control of others that they were able to dominate and destroy.

The Laws of Wickedness

God has commanded us to "suffer not that these murderous combinations shall get above you,"[69] so how ought we to discharge that obligation? To answer that question, we must ask what the anti-Christs conspire to accomplish. First and foremost, their goal is to obtain positions of political power to ensure that their like-minded cohorts "should not suffer for their murders, and their plunderings, and their stealings."[70] Being able to legally justify immoral, un-Christian conduct helps the anti-Christs perpetuate and consolidate power over others. Secret combinations do not take down the government by attacking it from the sidelines; they gut it from within.

Those involved in this effort work to circumvent "the laws of their country" to instead carry on their nefarious deeds "according to the laws of their wickedness."[71] They "[let] the guilty and the wicked go unpunished because of their money." And they are "held in office at the head of government,

67. Doctrine and Covenants 38:29.
68. Joseph L. Wirthlin, in Conference Report, October 1946.
69. Ether 8:23.
70. Helaman 6:21.
71. Helaman 6:24.

to rule and do according to their wills."[72] Of course, this is one of the primary features of Caesar—the institutionalization of conduct that would be widely considered immoral and unjust if done by one person directly against another. Consider how governments use coercively-taken taxpayer dollars to financially absolve specific businesses and industries from the consequences of their actions. Social welfare laws steal property from some to give to others. Governments use electronic surveillance to spy on people. They torture individuals labeled "enemy combatants" to make them seem subhuman or incarcerate people because they ingested a forbidden plant. These same governments can assassinate individuals suspected of misconduct, sexually molest people who simply wish to travel on a plane, steal wealth from future generations by creating new money that inflates the money supply, and on and on.

Satan has long sought to undermine agency, including by enabling people to (try to) avoid the consequences of their actions—the "eat, drink, and be merry"[73] option. Lucifer and his mortal minions tell us we can commit sin and still "be saved in the kingdom of God."[74] Satan encourages people to follow him so they can do what they want to do and be held guiltless. It is the promise given to Cain,[75] and it is the offer that seduces all who belong to the devil's church. Caesar is merely a mortal manifestation through which these temptations play out, inviting God's children to participate in the process. The Book of Mormon describes how the influential minority that comprised the secret combination carried on a propaganda campaign whereby they "seduced the more part of the righteous until they had come down to believe in their works and partake of their spoils, and to join with them in their secret murders and combinations."[76] In other words, the people welcomed with open arms, and elected to various offices of power, individuals who enabled them in their wickedness and protected them in their evil desires through the "laws of their wickedness" that purported to legally justify wrongful conduct. Not wishing to be governed by God's law and be held accountable for their wickedness, they embraced a corrupt system that justified them in their deviant behavior and sanctioned their wickedness.

Only with the broad support of the masses were the secret combinations, composed of a tiny minority of individuals, able to "obtain the sole

72. Helaman 7:5.
73. 2 Nephi 28:8.
74. Ibid.
75. Moses 5:30–31.
76. Helaman 6:38.

management of the government."[77] This is not to say, of course, that everyone explicitly supported power-seeking murderers and consciously sanctioned plundering to enrich themselves. Rather, those who "[partook] of their spoils" likely believed it was part of the process. Caesar normalizes his activities to the point that terms like social safety net, stimulus, bailout, and welfare lose any negative connotation and instead become acceptable, if not praiseworthy. The spoils of Caesar include the political process itself that allows individuals to control their peers, such as taxing others to fund a park or building or program that only some desire, dictating how others' property can be used in order to manipulate and protect the perceived "value" of their own property, or making others pay for their own children's education. It could likewise be argued that the majority of people also "join with them in their secret murders," in part, by supporting an aggressive "foreign policy" that involves the intentional killing of innocent people. Those who collude with Caesar are not immune from his actions. Just as the Gadianton Robbers tempted the broader public into benefitting from the results of their evil actions, those who support the state and benefit from its programs have been seduced and ought to reconsider.

Anything short of the gospel of Jesus Christ appears to be insufficient to stop Lucifer, or Caesar, or secret combinations. It was the Lamanites who "did preach the word of God among the more wicked part of them, insomuch that this band of robbers was utterly destroyed."[78] The Book of Mormon's lesson is clear: Satan's long-standing effort to avoid consequences for evil behavior continues today. The state, through which he operates, similarly seduces people to partake in Caesar's spoils and uphold those who substitute the laws of wickedness for God's law.

Taxation Is Theft

Caesar is not cheap—his programs and policies require revenue to sustain and implement. Governments have thus typically turned to taxation to finance their operations, coercing the many to support the decisions of the few, which (ostensibly) benefit the many. This money is not freely given, of course; taxation is inherently plunderous. Any demand for a tax payment is predicated on a fist or firearm backing up the request.

77. Helaman 6:39.
78. Helaman 6:37.

The Book of Mormon shares this cynical view of Caesar's revenue-generating scheme. Consider King Noah, who "did not keep the commandments of God" but "did walk after the desires of his own heart."[79] Part of his "whoredoms and . . . wickedness"[80] were that "he laid a tax of one fifth part of all [his subjects] possessed"[81]—a 20% tax, which financed public works projects[82] and personal aggrandizement.[83] The king and his cronies "were supported in their laziness, and in their idolatry, and in their whoredoms"[84] by these taxes. Mormon's assessment of the situation is as succinct as it is scathing: "thus did the people labor exceedingly to support iniquity."[85] Lucifer's desire is to buy power with the treasures he takes from those he controls. Taxes finance military forces, police officers, prisons, large bureaucracies that restrict people's freedom, and more—institutionalizing injustice and making those affected finance it.

Of course, it got worse for King Noah's subjects. They were invaded by the Lamanites and, as war captives, forced to "pay tribute to the king of the Lamanites" an annual payment of "one half of all they possessed."[86] This heavy taxation was designed "for the sole purpose of bringing this people into subjection or into bondage." And the taxes were indeed perceived as bondage, for as their new leader, Limhi, complained, "one half of all we have or possess the king of the Lamanites doth exact of us, *or our lives*."[87] It was not just about making an annoying, large payment; it was a literal strangulation of their lives and livelihoods by the controlling Caesar of the time. "Is not this grievous to be borne?" Limhi continued. "And is not this, our affliction, great? Now behold, how great reason we have to mourn."[88] Far from painting taxes as something benign such as "the price we pay for a civilized society,"[89] the Book of Mormon paints them—at least in this story—as a mechanism for bondage and the result of wickedness.

Consider the story of Riplakish, another wicked ruler who "did not do that which was right in the sight of the Lord, for he . . . did lay that

79. Mosiah 11:2.
80. Ibid.
81. Mosiah 11:3.
82. Mosiah 11:8.
83. Mosiah 11:6.
84. Ibid.
85. Ibid.
86. Mosiah 19:15.
87. Mosiah 7:22; emphasis added.
88. Mosiah 7:23.
89. "Taxes Are What We Pay for Civilized Society," Quote Investigator, accessed April 25, 2020, https://quoteinvestigator.com/2012/04/13/taxes-civilize/.

upon men's shoulders which was grievous to be borne"—a term Moroni, summarizing the Jaredite record, no doubt used after seeing Limhi use it centuries earlier. What was not "right in the sight of the Lord," per scripture? "[Riplakish] did tax them with heavy taxes."[90] Caesar has to deal with those who prefer to keep their property rather than have it taken, so as with all other state officials extorting their subjects, Riplakish "did build many prisons, and whoso would not be subject unto taxes he did cast into prison; and whoso was not able to pay taxes he did cast into prison."[91] This tax-generation scheme was the central component by which the king "did afflict the people with his whoredoms and abominations." Such a scheme is not only unsupported by scripture, it is condemned as going against the Lord's will.

Contrast these stories with that of Benjamin, a righteous ruler who evidently levied no taxes at all and is presented as a virtuous model of leadership for readers to emulate—a king "more in name than in fact."[92] He reminded his fellow Nephites that he had "not sought gold nor silver nor any manner of riches of you."[93] Instead, in total contrast to the typical Caesarean tax regime, "even I, myself, have labored with mine own hands that I might serve you, and that ye should not be laden with taxes," he said, "that there should nothing come upon you which was grievous to be borne."[94] And since taxes inevitably lead to punishment for those who fail to pay up, the king likewise pointed out that he had not permitted "that ye should be confined in dungeons . . . nor that ye should . . . plunder, or steal."[95] He did this by refusing to set the bad example himself. Later in his life, he reminded his peers of how he had lived so that he could "answer a clear conscience before God,"[96] reinforcing the idea that taxation—the forcible taking of property from others, backed by the threat or use of force—is a sin that is not "right in the sight of the Lord."

In the so-called "land of liberty,"[97] individuals pay taxes on their income, businesses, property, inheritance, capital gains, retail purchases, recreation, gifts, retirement, fuel, food, phones, and more, to say nothing of the fees paid for building permits, business permits, vehicle registrations, marriage licenses,

---

90. Ether 10:5.
91. Ether 10:6.
92. Orson Pratt, in *Journal of Discourses*, vol. 23 (Liverpool: John Henry Smith, 1883)
90. He goes on to say that he was more akin to a patriarch or father to the people.
93. Mosiah 2:12.
94. Mosiah 2:14.
95. Mosiah 2:13.
96. Mosiah 2:15.
97. 2 Nephi 1:7.

hunting licenses, animal licenses, and on and on. Americans collectively spend more each year on taxes than they do "on food, clothing, and housing—combined," and spend, on average, over one-third of the year working enough to pay for all of these ongoing demands.[98] Truly what Caesar exacts of us, or our *lives*, is a heavy toll, and as the key figures in the Book of Mormon state, each time taxes are mentioned, such a burden is "grievous to be borne."

The Ideal

In scripture, often a wicked ruler prompts God to send a prophet to call the ruler and the people to repentance. Such was the case during King Noah's reign when the Lord told Abinadi "go and prophesy unto this my people, for they have hardened their hearts against my words; they have repented not of their evil doings."[99] His message predictably fell upon largely deaf ears. But a priest named Alma "believed the words which Abinadi had spoken, for he knew concerning the iniquity which Abinadi had testified against them."[100] Driven out of his society for daring to defy the king,[101] Alma began preaching privately to people,[102] building a community of 450 people who ultimately fled deep[103] into the wilderness after the king "sent his army to destroy them."[104] This new community, with no Caesar to coordinate and control their activities, began developing infrastructure and agriculture, living in peace and pursuing prosperity, yet soon they became "desirous that Alma should be their king."[105] And, following the pattern of prior prophets, Alma protested:

> Behold, it is not expedient that we should have a king; for thus saith the Lord: Ye shall not esteem one flesh above another, or one man shall not think himself above another; therefore I say unto you it is not expedient that ye should have a king.
>
> And now I say unto you, ye have been oppressed by king Noah, and have been in bondage to him and his priests, and have been brought into iniquity by them; therefore ye were bound with the bands of iniquity.

98. "Tax Freedom Day 2019 is April 16th," Tax Foundation, April 10, 2019, https://taxfoundation.org/publications/tax-freedom-day/.
99. Mosiah 12:1.
100. Mosiah 17:2.
101. Mosiah 17:3.
102. Mosiah 18:1–3.
103. Mosiah 23:3.
104. Mosiah 18:31–34.
105. Mosiah 23:5–6.

> And now as ye have been delivered by the power of God out of these bonds; yea, even out of the hands of king Noah and his people, and also from the bonds of iniquity, even so I desire that ye should stand fast in this liberty wherewith ye have been made free, and that ye trust no man to be a king over you.[106]

He also pointed out that the deficiency in mortal men ruling over one another is that you cannot "always have just men"[107] holding such power over others—something Mosiah later argued.[108] Further, the "iniquity" of such rulers creates a "snare" leading people to do "many things which [are] abominable in the sight of the Lord."[109] But Alma's central argument for rejecting a kingship is that Christ commands us to "not esteem one flesh above another," echoing the Golden Rule's fundamental mandate of love and of treating others as we would ourselves wish to be treated. Mosiah echoed this when he taught that "every man should esteem his neighbor as himself, laboring with their own hands for their support"[110]—a call that inherently undermines Caesar's taxation and welfare systems. And the Lord has likewise said, "let every man esteem his brother as himself," considering it sufficiently important to immediately repeat the counsel a second time.[111] It was this sin of pride—through which "we are tempted daily to elevate ourselves above others and diminish them"[112]—that caused the fall of the Book of Mormon peoples.[113]

We have been warned to avoid pride lest we fall prey to the same outcome.[114] Part of our temptation to participate in this pride stems from being subjected to Caesar, whose entire existence depends on subordinating others beneath himself. This is evident in the pattern of Satan's supporters who seek to "be lifted up one above another"[115] by acquiring wealth and power. The state facilitates one favored group's domination over others, whether it be a king and his subjects, or victorious voters coercing the defeated minority to submit to their will. The iniquity of mortal men ruling over one another is the snare that leads people to do abominable things.

---

106. Mosiah 23:7, 12–13.
107. Mosiah 23:8.
108. Mosiah 29:16.
109. Mosiah 23:9.
110. Mosiah 27:4.
111. Doctrine and Covenants 38:24–25.
112. Ezra Taft Benson, "Beware of Pride," *Ensign*, May 1989.
113. Moroni 8:27;
114. Doctrine and Covenants 38:39.
115. Helaman 6:17; see also 2 Nephi 24:13–14.

It is instructive to note that by rejecting such a snare and abdicating any claim to secular rule over his peers, Alma set up his small society to "stand fast in this liberty wherewith ye have been made free."[116] Alma thereby established a contrast between bondage and mortal rule on the one hand, and liberty and self-rule on the other—a contrast that permeates the Book of Mormon. Alma does not remind his followers of all the supposed benefits that come from Caesar: protection from enemies, public works, personal financial benefits, and so forth. Rather, he urges them to remember when they were "bound with the bands of iniquity"[117] and the injustices that caused. Alma portrays the state not as a provider of resources and benefits, or even a necessary evil, but rather an evil to be avoided.

Contrary to the other societies described in the Book of Mormon, Alma's people were persuaded to abandon their desires for a Caesar and effectively lived under self-rule for a period of time. During that period the people "began to prosper exceedingly."[118] The claim that a self-ruling governance model is impractical is thus proven invalid. Indeed, even when the system of judges was overtaken by secret combinations[119] and various tribes broke off from the would-be dictatorship to govern themselves,[120] Mormon records that the decentralized groups "had peace in the land." This peace persisted despite the fact that these groups did not choose to adopt a system of governance whereby God's law, given via Moses, would guide their affairs.[121] This alternative model of self-rule, even when used by those who "were not a righteous people,"[122] still produced favorable outcomes when compared to the iniquity, bondage, and captivity that comes with Caesar.

The same result is evident in the case of the Nephites who witnessed Jesus's visit to the Americas. This community of faithful Christians were so committed to the gospel that they experienced "no contentions and disputations, and every man did deal justly one with another."[123] No longer a tribal society, this group "did not walk any more after the performances and ordinances of the law of Moses; but they did walk after the commandments which they had received from their Lord and their God"[124]

116. Mosiah 23:13.
117. Mosiah 23:12.
118. Mosiah 23:19–20.
119. 3 Nephi 7:1–2.
120. 3 Nephi 7:9–11.
121. 3 Nephi 7:14.
122. 3 Nephi 7:11.
123. 4 Nephi 1:2.
124. 4 Nephi 1:12.

and enjoyed a prolonged period[125] of self-rule, with Christ as their only king. Consequently, "the Lord did prosper them exceedingly"[126] and "they were all made free," a phrase that once again reinforces the contrast with Caesar's captivity.

The Book of Mormon goes to great lengths to emphasize the dangers of government and the bondage that comes when mortal rulers, supported by Satan, impose their designs on others. These examples present an ideal alternative, one in which individuals submit to Christ and are only ruled by Him. If indeed this scripture is "inspired and inspiring concerning the solutions of [today's] problems,"[127] it therefore follows that these circumstances ought to be aspired to by every committed Christian. Because we cannot "esteem one flesh above another," we must reject Caesar.

Our Condemnation

The Bible is a compilation of apostolic documents and letters that circulated independently from one another for hundreds of years before finally being compiled into the book we know today. Over time, plain and precious truths were omitted from the records in order to "pervert the right ways of the Lord" and "blind the eyes and harden the hearts of the children of men."[128] It is harder for Christians to remain sufficiently faithful if their theological text is watered down, or key passages omitted. They have therefore long been left to "stumble exceedingly" because important portions of the gospel "have been kept back by that abominable church"[129]—the whore of Babylon. Of course, Lucifer thrives best in ignorance; when people are unaware of his motives and operations, they are ill equipped to defend themselves against him. Thus he deceives[130] people that "there is no hell; and he saith unto them: I am no devil, for there is none."[131] His corrupt Caesars follow suit, for when their true nature is hidden and they are instead perceived as benevolent providers and protectors, people are seduced into participating in their processes and partaking of their spoils.[132] The

125. This was over 160 years; see 4 Nephi 1:24–26.
126. 4 Nephi 1:7.
127. Gordon B. Hinckley, "An Angel from on High, the Long, Long Silence Broke," *Ensign*, November 1979."
128. 1 Nephi 13:27.
129. 1 Nephi 13:34.
130. Alma 30:53; Jacob 7:18; 3 Nephi 1:22; Doctrine and Covenants 50:3; 52:14;
131. 2 Nephi 28:22.
132. Helaman 6:38.

Bible, stripped of its more plain and precious truths, has been unable to help Christians sufficiently see why Caesar and his master must both be rejected.

The "whole world [groaned] under darkness,"[133] stumbling on forbidden paths,[134] but the Lord wanted to "restore his people from their lost and fallen state"[135] so He "[proceeded] to do a marvellous work,"[136] the restoration of "much of [His] gospel, which [is] plain and precious."[137] This was done specifically because people were stumbling without scriptural clarity, not just about strictly theological issues, but also because of the influence of the adversary. The Book of Mormon empowers its readers with relevant and actionable knowledge about the problems with mortal rule. Those with eyes to see can see a message that is largely omitted from the Bible, and even, sadly, escapes the attention and understanding of many who claim to believe that the Book of Mormon is additional scripture. While pointing our attention to Christ,[138] the book also strips us of our ignorance—if we let it—regarding how Satan uses mortal men and their organizations to advance his agenda. We are consequently to "do that which [is] right in the sight of the Lord,"[139] not "esteem one flesh above another,"[140] and "suffer not that [secret] combinations shall get above [us]."[141] And we are further told to

> waste and wear out our lives in bringing to light all the hidden things of darkness, wherein we know them; and they are truly manifest from heaven—
>
> These should then be attended to with great earnestness.
>
> Let no man count them as small things; for there is much which lieth in futurity, pertaining to the saints, which depends upon these things.[142]

The Book of Mormon is the primary vehicle through which the Lord has empowered us to "discover . . . the works of [our] brethren, yea, their secret works, their works of darkness, and their wickedness and abominations."[143] Those who are entrusted with this marvelous work have an "imperative duty" to enlighten others with its plain and precious truths of Christ, and its admonitions about His

---

133. Doctrine and Covenants 84:49.
134. 1 Nephi 8:28; 12:17.
135. 2 Nephi 25:17.
136. Isaiah 29:14.
137. 1 Nephi 13:34.
138. 2 Nephi 25:26.
139. Ether 10:5.
140. Mosiah 23:7.
141. Ether 8:23.
142. Doctrine and Covenants 123:13–15.
143. Alma 37:23, 25.

adversary, for "there are many yet on the earth . . . who are blinded by the subtle craftiness of men, whereby they lie in wait to deceive, and who are only kept from the truth because they know not where to find it."[144] Simply put, the Book of Mormon's existence obliges the reader to fully—and not simply superficially—understand it, and then to share it. Unfortunately, Latter-day Saints have failed:

> And your minds in times past have been darkened because of unbelief, and because you have treated lightly the things you have received—
>
> Which vanity and unbelief have brought the whole church under condemnation.
>
> And this condemnation resteth upon the children of Zion, even all.
>
> And they shall remain under this condemnation until they repent and remember the new covenant, even the Book of Mormon and the former commandments which I have given them, not only to say, but to do according to that which I have written.[145]

This condemnation has not been lifted.[146] It exists because we have "treated lightly" the warnings in the Book of Mormon by failing to even "remember" them. Certainly this does not mean that readers have failed to superficially recall information they previously read in the book. Instead, the usage of the term in the scriptures suggests that *remembering* is implicitly tied to action. Benjamin outlined to his sons the afflictions their ancestors suffered by "to stir them up in remembrance of their duty,"[147] not merely to put the historical knowledge in their minds. Helaman's sons "did remember his words; and therefore they went forth, keeping the commandments of God."[148] A recurring theme in the scriptures highlights the connection between remembering and keeping God's commandments.[149] In the Book of Mormon, the act of remembering means honoring the terms of God's covenant.[150]

We cannot remember that which we do not learn, so reading God's "marvelous work"[151] is an obvious prerequisite. There are many "who are very careless about reading the Book of Mormon . . . who suffer this book to remain

144. Doctrine and Covenants 123:11–12.
145. Doctrine and Covenants 84:54–57.
146. "Some of us may not live long enough to see the day when the Book of Mormon floods the earth and when the Lord lifts His condemnation." Ezra Taft Benson, "Flooding the Earth with the Book of Mormon," *Ensign*, November 1988.
147. Mosiah 1:17.
148. Helaman 5:14.
149. Deuteronomy 5:12; Exodus 20:8; Jarom 1:5; Mosiah 18:23.
150. 1 Nephi 2:24; Alma 37:13; Mosiah 1:5–7.
151. 3 Nephi 21:9.

upon their shelves, week after week, without ever reading a page of these precious things."[152] But it is not enough merely to read it, or even to focus solely on its spiritually uplifting gospel messages. We must also remember its warnings and lessons, not so we can simply say we agree with its message, but rather so we can *do* as the book directs. After all, "our families may be corrupted by worldly trends and teachings unless we know how to use the book to expose and combat falsehoods."[153] We must "read and heed the words of God and quit building up and upholding secret combinations."[154] We have to "be so familiar with the scriptures themselves that [we] not only recognize the solutions, but also understand and apply them to current questions and problems."[155] Those who do not learn from the past are *condemned* to repeat it—an outcome the Book of Mormon was written to prevent.

The "vanity" that contributes to our condemnation is a "fruitless desire or endeavor,"[156] which comes because "we insist upon following the culture of the world" and as Christians therefore "try to live the impossible"[157]—attempting to serve two masters, Christ and a counterfeit Caesar together. We "find excessive self-satisfaction in thinking that both God and the world are pleased with us,"[158] engaged in behavior to be "like all the nations,"[159] while simultaneously claiming to still be part of a "peculiar people."[160] Pitted between two polar opposites, too many among us try to find a common ground between Christ and Caesar, hoping to blend the two. But it is vain to be "lukewarm, and neither cold nor hot;"[161] we must choose one way or the other.[162] Because God wants to be the sole object of our worship and loyalty,[163] a Christian who supports Caesar is therefore not fully Christian.

---

152. Orson Pratt, as quoted in "Orson Pratt: Early Advocate of the Book of Mormon," *Ensign*, April 1984.
153. Ezra Taft Benson, "The Book of Mormon Is the Word of God," *Ensign*, January 1988.
154. Ibid.
155. Marion G. Romney, address to seminary and institute personnel, BYU, July 13, 1970, 5.
156. "Vanity," American Dictionary of the English Language, accessed May 2, 2020, http://webstersdictionary1828.com/Dictionary/vanity.
157. "What is the condemnation we are under that President Benson speaks of regarding the Book of Mormon?," *Ensign*, February 1991.
158. Ibid.
159. 1 Samuel 8:20.
160. Exodus 19:5.
161. Revelation 3:16.
162. Joshua 24:15.
163. Exodus 34:14.

What we often forget is that the Book of Mormon contains only a limited portion of what God wishes us to understand. The Lord revealed that it contains "much of [His] gospel,"[164] but not all, as it represents only the "lesser part" of what Jesus taught.[165] Past prophets were "forbidden" to document a great number of things, even "all things," that were sealed up to be revealed "in their purity" at some later time.[166] We have been invited to see "the greater things, the knowledge of which is hid up because of unbelief,"[167] but we can only access them if we "believe [the lesser part]"[168] first. Because we have treated the lesser things lightly, not even using them to their full and intended extent, "the greater things [are] withheld from [us], unto [our] condemnation."[169] As a result of "the wickedness and abominations of the people," the sealed portion has not been revealed. Yet the lesser portion, the Book of Mormon, helps its readers understand how to avoid and overcome such wickedness and abominations. If we do not use what God has given, why would He give us more?

Despite the amazing messages and important warnings in this additional witness of Christ, most of its readers seem to be seduced by Caesar. Secret combinations are as intertwined with the state today as they were when they infected the Nephite and Jaredite governments. Book of Mormon readers generally cannot identify such forces and therefore are completely unable to "suffer not"[170] that they get above us. We are governed by "laws of wickedness" under that which is "grievous to be borne," yet we refuse to reject Caesar in favor of Christ. We have been invited to "flood the earth with the Book of Mormon"[171]—out of recognition that we must lift the condemnation we are under. This first requires remembering and acting based on what we have already been taught. Satan and his mortal minions succeed when we fail to heed scriptural warnings about them. There are many who "[profess] to know the Christ, and yet [who] deny the more parts of his gospel, insomuch that they . . . receive all manner of wickedness."[172] The Book of Mormon invites us to know Christ and embrace His gospel fully, including by believing it sufficiently to obtain even more revelation from God. The choice is up to us.

---

164. 1 Nephi 13:34–35.
165. 3 Nephi 26:8–11; Mormon 8:12.
166. Ether 4:4–7; 13:13; 1 Nephi 14:26–28; 2 Nephi 27:10; 3 Nephi 26:11; Doctrine and Covenants 93:6–18.
167. Ether 4:13; 1 Nephi 13:40; Doctrine and Covenants 6:26.
168. 3 Nephi 26:9.
169. 3 Nephi 26:10.
170. Ether 8:23.
171. Ezra Taft Benson, "Flooding the Earth with the Book of Mormon," *Ensign*, November 1988.
172. 4 Nephi 1:27.

CAESAR AS COUNTERFEIT

To know Christ is to reject His counterfeit. Just as a person cannot be sure they have legitimate currency without understanding what a fake might look like, we cannot be confident in our discipleship if we do not know who the "false Christs, and false prophets" might be that Jesus warned about. And, perhaps more importantly, we must know what such imposters wish to impose upon the deceived masses. Recognizing a counterfeit is necessary in order to then reject it.

Throughout time there have been many who "professed to know the Christ" yet "deny the more parts of his gospel, insomuch that they . . . receive all manner of wickedness."[1] The natural man[2] appears susceptible to this trend; many self-proclaimed Christians fail to "endure sound doctrine; but after their own lusts . . . they heap to themselves teachers, having itching ears."[3] It is seemingly easy to be appeased with a counterfeit Christ, a watered-down gospel in which we accommodate Caesar, and thus Satan, to varying degrees. We render unto Caesar far more than he is due and blind ourselves to our attempts to serve two masters, thinking instead that service to Christ can include our support for Caesar. So-called "patriotism" becomes assimilated into our religious expression, and we replace God's law with Caesarean policies and programs "like all the nations,"[4] enticed by the

1. 4 Nephi 1:27.
2. Mosiah 3:19.
3. 2 Timothy 4:3.
4. 1 Samuel 8:5.

arm of flesh.[5] What's most alarming is that, like any effective counterfeit, the masses do not see Caesar's deceptions for what they actually are. Satan's goal "to deceive and to blind men"[6] is realized through these counterfeits, leading people away from the Lord.

It is not easy to share such a message, nor is it easy for many to receive it. Those who have contaminated their Christianity with Caesar's schemes might take "the truth to be hard, for it cutteth them to the very center."[7] It is not surprising to see people resist when told that their conception of true Christianity is incorrect. Consider the fictional story of *The Matrix*, in which humanity has been plugged into a dream world to deceive them into not realizing the truth: that they are slaves to a system using them for its own purposes. Morpheus helps Neo distinguish between the real world and the virtual as they pass through a crowd of people, representing those who are in the Matrix—people who were raised within a counterfeit reality and do not know any different. Neo himself was part of this reality until Morpheus rescued him and shared the truth. "You have to understand," Morpheus explains, "that most of these people . . . are so inured, so hopelessly dependent on the system, that they will fight to protect it."[8] Such is commonly the case with Christians who have embraced Caesar's corrupt counterfeits. Tell a "Christian conservative," for example, that his feverish support for the military or reverence of the flag might constitute idolatry, and you are likely to be called some colorful (and unchristian) names. Suggest to a public schooling parent that the institution is an indoctrination system for Caesarean supporters, and you will no doubt be attacked.

But we cannot adequately pursue the truth unless we clearly see what is false. Once awoken to the truth, we are not justified in condemning those who remain asleep in deception, continuing to accommodate Caesar in their worship of Christ. If anything, we should be further motivated to help others "awake from a deep sleep, yea, even from the sleep of hell, and shake off the awful chains by which [they] are bound."[9] But if we wish to worship Christ, we need to know, and avoid, the many ways that the Deceiver tries to divert our loyalty and attention—even if they are commonly supported and socially popularized and reinforced.

---

5. Doctrine and Covenants 1:19.
6. Moses 4:4.
7. 1 Nephi 16:2.
8. *The Matrix*, directed by Andy Wachowski and Larry Wachowski (Warner Bros. Pictures, 1999).
9. 2 Nephi 1:13.

Many Christians are aware of the concept of the antichrist, introduced first by the apostle John.[10] But while knowing that "the great antichrist is Lucifer," most do not understand that "he has many assistants both as spirit beings and as mortals."[11] His work is not merely an end-of-times apocalyptic showdown, set for some distant day,[12] but an ongoing campaign to daily deceive and divert us away from Christ. The antichrist is "anyone or anything that counterfeits the true gospel or plan of salvation."[13] But this is not easily evident to the Christian masses, because like any counterfeiters aiming to pass off their deception as legitimate and true, Caesar's servants and supporters are passed off, and often perceived, as "ministers of righteousness."[14] We see as harmless, or even beneficial, that which competes against Christ. We embrace the enemy, often with enough cognitive dissonance to not even recognize what we are actually doing.

Spotting a "fake" becomes easier when someone helps you focus on the specific characteristics of the counterfeit that, once seen, cannot be unseen. Armed with this knowledge, you can more readily distinguish a deception from the truth. What, then, are some of Caesar's counterfeits that, once understood, can empower us with helpful, discerning knowledge for the future?

Flattery

Before discussing some specifics about Caesar's common counterfeits, we need to understand one of his primary tactics in deceiving us into trying to serve both him and Christ together—with his ultimate goal being, of course, that we serve only him. Observations and warnings about Satan's chief tactic permeate the scriptures, yet in scattered isolation these references may not make apparent how central this tactic is to his goals. Bringing it to focus here will help us more readily understand how Caesar's counterfeits attain such popularity, and why they are to be avoided. This tactic is flattery.

Simply put, flattery is gratification by falsification, and in that sense, it is itself a counterfeit. While God wants us to experience joy and feel His love,[15] the adversary offers a cheapened alternative that is without substance

10. 1 John 2:18–22; 4:3–6; 2 John 1:7.
11. "Antichrist," Bible Dictionary, https://www.churchofjesuschrist.org/study/scriptures/bd/antichrist.
12. 2 Thessalonians 2:4.
13. "Antichrist," ibid.
14. 2 Corinthians 11:15.
15. 2 Nephi 2:25; Alma 5:26.

or sincerity. Flattery is "the raising of false and unfounded hopes; there is always an element of dishonesty attending it."[16] Satan makes false promises, such as telling Jesus he could give Him the "kingdoms of the world, and the glory of them" if only Jesus worshiped him.[17] Likewise, Caesar promises that which he cannot offer. Everything he does is through theft, coercion, and deception. He takes from some to give to others, portraying himself as a savior while he is nothing more than a corrupt middleman. He raises our hopes of security and prosperity,[18] but only God can provide these things.[19]

Those who employ flattery do so through deception; they are false in their communication, but they must trick the hearer into believing they are sincere. Lucifer lured countless numbers of God's children with the promise of consequence-free living and eventual salvation—the ability to "eat, drink, and be merry" while being saved in sin.[20] He flattered his subjects by appealing to their vanity, providing a false hope that he could not deliver. His tool of flattery is similarly employed on earth,[21] because "he knows the great power of speech"[22] and its ability to deceive the masses.

Throughout scripture, flattery is associated with deception, vanity, and idolatry; it is an effective tool to distract Christians and lead them into attempting to serve two masters at once, often unwittingly. This persuasive speech is portrayed as a deceptive skill, enabling a person to lead others toward a desired end. For Satan, this desired end is for us to worship a counterfeit Christ and embrace a false gospel. Secret combinations of bygone eras were seductive because they appeared alluring; the promise of power and wealth were cloaked in flattery to hide their true, authoritarian agenda, which necessarily includes harm to others. In our own day, similar agendas are masked behind a facade of false intentions—an outward portrayal of patriotism and do-goodery that deceives the public into supporting Caesar's true mission and the master he serves. The Psalmist described the problem well:

> He has put forth his hands against those who were at peace with him;
> He has violated his covenant.
> His speech was smoother than butter,

16. Bruce R. McConkie, *Mormon Doctrine* (Salt Lake City: Bookcraft, 1979), 287.
17. Matthew 4:9.
18. 2 Nephi 28:21; Helaman 6:21; Isaiah 2:8; Moses 5:31.
19. Psalm 20:7; 2 Chronicles 32:8; Jeremiah 17:5; 2 Nephi 28:31; Doctrine and Covenants 1:19
20. 2 Nephi 28:7–8.
21. 2 Nephi 28:22.
22. James E. Faust, "The Great Imitator," *Ensign*, November 1987.

But his heart was war;
His words were softer than oil,
Yet they were drawn swords.[23]

Job recognized the dangers of flattery,[24] and Daniel described foreign foes who "[corrupted] by flatteries"[25] God's people, leading them into idolatry. Paul avoided it entirely.[26] To the Romans, he pointed out that for those who cause dissension among the followers of Christ, "by their smooth and flattering speech they deceive the hearts of the unsuspecting."[27] Pahoran described rebels who "used great flattery" to lead away "the hearts of many people."[28] The charismatic Sherem "had a perfect knowledge of the language of the people; wherefore, he could use much flattery, and much power of speech"[29] to deceive others into embracing counterfeit doctrine. The idolatrous priests of King Noah used "vain and flattering words"[30] to encourage their people in wickedness. Korihor employed this tactic to "[lead] away the hearts of many,"[31] as did Amalickiah and Gadianton.[32]

There are many who "teach after this manner, false and vain and foolish doctrines."[33] Flattery "often sounds so reasonable and [the] message so easy to justify. It is an appealing, intriguing voice with dulcet tones."[34] We want to believe it because it raises our hopes (albeit falsely) and makes promises we find tempting. Is it any doubt that Caesar takes full advantage of flattery? Those seeking Caesar's power campaign on flattering messages like ending and avoiding wars, only to launch new ones, or escalate existing ones. They tell us there will be "no new taxes" only to raise existing taxes and add new ones. They give false promises of peace and prosperity, yet both slip away as we place our hopes in Caesar instead of Christ. We are told what we want to hear by those who want to obtain power over us. "Of those men who have overturned" our God-given liberty, "the greatest number have begun their career by paying an obsequious court to the people . . . commencing

---

23. Psalm 55:20–21.
24. Job 32:21–22.
25. Daniel 11:32.
26. 1 Thessalonians 2:5.
27. Romans 16:18; New American Standard Bible.
28. Alma 61:4.
29. Jacob 7:4.
30. Mosiah 11:7.
31. Alma 30:18.
32. Alma 46:10; Helaman 2:4.
33. 2 Nephi 28:9.
34. Faust, "The Great Imitator."

demagogues, and ending tyrants."[35] This follows Satan's model, used by his secret combinations on earth, whereby "he leadeth them by the neck with a flaxen cord, until he bindeth them with his strong cords forever."[36] Chains are not enticing to the masses, but a long, loose leash can be, when accompanied with alleged benefits. That leash is self-imposed in many cases as our attention and affection are so often directed to mortal institutions as perceived providers and protectors, leading us to increasingly forsake God. Caesar's counterfeits and Satan's seductions tempt us away from being faithful by deceiving us into following false gods and a counterfeit plan of salvation. The "flattery of the tongue of a strange woman"[37] entices us, leading us to be unfaithful to the Bridegroom.[38]

Christians face several threats from a persistent adversary, including flattery.[39] Caesar bombards us with false promises and encourages us to employ his claimed power selfishly for our own gain. If we want the city to build a soccer field near us, or do not like a neighbor's use of their property, or want to raise everyone's taxes to help fund a program we like, we find encouragement everywhere—and justification aplenty—to side with Caesar. Such use of the state is normalized and popularized. And our participation in the process is cheered on with flattery such as our being part of "the will of the majority," or "making a difference," or "being a good citizen," or "exercising our right to vote." We are praised for participating in the "civic sacrament"[40] of using Caesar's power against others, continually compromising ourselves as Christians each time we use such a process to violate Christ's commandment to love one another.

It is easy to read ancient examples of spiritually misguided societies and see where they went astray. We pity or scorn those who fell prey to Caesar's counterfeits and Satan's snares. We chide people in times past for being so easily enticed by those who sought power over them. But living in the middle of the same patterns, how do we fare? Christians condemn the children of Israel for their rampant idolatry, yet by and large they fail to

35. Alexander Hamilton, in *The Federalist* (Chicago: Scott, Foresman and Company, 1894), 13.
36. 2 Nephi 26:22.
37. Proverbs 6:24.
38. Doctrine and Covenants 65:3.
39. Joseph F. Smith, as quoted in Ezra Taft Benson, in Conference Report, October 1964. Smith said: "There are at least three dangers that threaten the Church within . . . flattery of prominent men in the world, false educational ideas, and sexual impurity."
40. "Election Day: Voting is our 'civic sacrament'," *The Christian Science Monitor*, November 5, 2012, https://www.csmonitor.com/Commentary/the-monitors-view/2012/1105/Election-Day-Voting-is-our-civic-sacrament.

recognize their own.[41] The person who is flattered has a hard time distinguishing deception from the truth. Amid these devilish deceptions, Caesar's counterfeits are passed off as praiseworthy, even among Christians.

Government Schools

There is no better way to deceive the masses than to control their most formative years of intellectual development. Adolf Hitler referenced the broader Caesarean campaign to capture the loyalties of the rising generation when he succinctly said, "He alone who owns the youth, gains the future."[42] He also said:

> When an opponent declares, "I will not come over to your side," I calmly say, "Your child belongs to us already . . . . What are you? You will pass on. Your descendants, however, now stand in the new camp. In a short time they will know nothing else but this new community."[43]

Just as Caesar wishes to supplant God as deity, he also positions himself as a substitute father for our Father in Heaven. The Roman senate would confer the title of father upon their imperial rulers; Augustus "wanted, more than any other image, to portray the Empire as *patria* [fatherland], himself as *pater patriae* [father of the fatherland], and the whole Roman people as children."[44] Julius instructed his subjects to "conduct yourselves toward me as toward a father." In turn, he told them he would "take thought for you as for my children."[45] This presumption of a parental relationship permeates today's legal systems. The legal doctrine of *parens patriae* (parent of the nation) is cited by government officials seeking to control the affairs of the young. Before English common law helped codify this legal doctrine in the seventeenth century, "the family's autonomy to do essentially as it saw fit with its children was untouched."[46] While an assertion of authority by the state might be justified in cases of

---

41. Mosiah 11:7.
42. Jennifer Keeley, *Life in the Hitler Youth* (San Diego: Lucent Books, 1999), 8–10.
43. William L. Shirer, *Rise And Fall Of The Third Reich: A History of Nazi Germany* (New York: Simon & Schuster, 1990), 249.
44. Abera M. Mengestu, *God as Father in Paul: Kinship Language and Identity Formation in Early Christianity* (Eugene: Pickwick Publications, 2013), 63.
45. Ibid, 61.
46. Marvin Ventrell, "The History of Child Welfare Law," *Child Welfare Law and Practice*, Case 117.

children being abused by their parents, it becomes extremely problematic when serving as the legal basis and philosophical framework to intervene unnecessarily into the parent-child relationship.

God commands parents to "bring up [their] children in light and truth."[47] The education of children is the natural responsibility of their parents.[48] But Caesar understands that the transmission of the religious and political ideas that form strong families inevitably creates a weak state; authoritarianism cannot survive, let alone flourish, in an environment of decentralized learning and free circulation of ideas.

There are two avenues to attack the parental responsibility of education. The first is through threats and coercion—restricting or entirely prohibiting parents from educating their children independently, as they best desire. Some judges assert that "there is no free-standing fundamental right of parents 'to control the upbringing of their children . . . in accordance with their personal and religious values and beliefs.' "[49] The US Supreme Court once similarly proclaimed that "the state has a wide range of power for limiting parental freedom and authority in things affecting the child's welfare."[50] These Caesarean structures are buttressed by academics and attorneys, as in the case of one outspoken Harvard law professor who argued for a "presumptive ban"[51] on parents educating their own children, suggesting that "some homeschooling parents are extreme religious ideologues who . . . hold views in serious conflict with those generally deemed central in our society" or that "many homeschooling parents are simply not capable of educating their children."[52] She also criticized parents assuming this responsibility for not sufficiently subjecting their children to the social whims of the majority:

> A very large proportion of homeschooling parents are ideologically committed to isolating their children from the majority culture and indoctrinating them in views and values that are in serious conflict with that culture.[53]

---

47. Doctrine and Covenants 93:40.
48. Deuteronomy 6:6–7.
49. *Fields v. Palmdale School District*, 427 F. 3d 1197.
50. *Prince v. Massachusetts*, 321 U.S. 158 (1944).
51. Erin O'Donnell, "The Risks of Homeschooling," *Harvard Magazine*, May–June 2020, https://harvardmagazine.com/2020/05/right-now-risks-homeschooling.
52. Elizabeth Bartholet, "Homeschooling: Parent Rights Absolutism vs. Child Rights to Education & Protection, *Arizona Law Review*, 62:1, https://arizonalawreview.org/pdf/62-1/62arizlrev1.pdf.
53. Ibid.

Others assert that parents have "no natural right to control their education fully"[54] and that Caesar's role in education "has served as a check on the power of parents, and this is another powerful reason for maintaining it."[55] Media pundits have piled on, audaciously arguing that "we have to break through our kind of private idea that kids belong to their parents, or kids belong to their families, and recognize that kids belong to whole communities."[56] Caesar's claim of political power over God's children gives rise to mandates and prohibitions that prevent parents from being the primary educators of their own kids.

This encroachment into education is often born out of animus against parents' religious beliefs and the political implications those beliefs can have. Caesar does not want children learning about his evils or about God, and thus he requires attendance at schools that omit such information. As one pastor said, Christians "cannot continue to send [their] children to Caesar for their education and be surprised when they come home as Romans."[57]

The second avenue to undermine the parental role in education is by assuming the responsibility from parents who willingly delegate it to the state. Many parents feel inferior to the task, prefer not to be around their children all day, or pursue employment out of the home and thus need the "free babysitting" that government schools effectively offer. In this system, children are filled with facts and sent home with hours of homework, eroding quality family time and imposing upon the natural bonds between parents and children. This cyclical process reinforces itself, as parents come to "trust the professionals" and assume that the curriculum is worthwhile, edifying, and a prerequisite for later success in life. This cycle becomes so culturally ingrained that its alternative is an anomaly; for decades, homeschooling was perceived to be anathema to the greater social order. In some countries it remains banned for that very reason. For example, the European Court of Human Rights affirmed a supposed "general interest of society to avoid the emergence of parallel societies based on separate philosophical convictions"[58] as the basis for denying parents the ability to avoid

---

54. Roger Soder, John I. Goodlad, and Timothy J. McMannon, eds., *Developing Democratic Character in the Young* (New York: Jossey-Bass, 2001), 164.
55. Ibid, 165.
56. "Melissa Harris-Perry Stands By Promo: 'Our Children Are Not Our Private Property'," *Huffington Post*, April 13, 2013, https://www.huffpost.com/entry/melissa-harris-perry-promo-children-msnbc_n_3076195.
57. Voddie Baucham Jr., *Family Driven Faith: Doing What It Takes to Raise Sons and Daughters Who Walk with God* (Wheaton: Crossway, 2007), 202.
58. "European Human Rights Court Upholds Nazi Ban on Homeschooling," *Brussels*

Caesar's schools and educate their own children. But the families pursuing this freedom are outliers; most families send their children to state schools, participate in its processes cheerfully, remain ignorant of its dangers, and structure their lives to justify their decisions—with each parent working outside the home, making themselves busy, and imagining that parenting their own children during most of the day is a nonstarter.

Caesar is, of course, eager to fill the void parents create for themselves, especially since there are such long-lasting implications in molding the minds of the young. This is not to say that the many who sustain the school system are knowingly complicit and ideologically ill-intentioned; most teachers are well-meaning and desire to communicate the knowledge they have studied. But they are part of a system that is inherently and institutionally counterfeit. Caesar's schools are systematically structured to cultivate a citizenry that is submissive to the state and ignorant of Caesar's illegitimacy. From their earliest days, government schools were political attempts to alter the social fabric of families. Horace Mann's "common school" concept in the 1830s was designed to reclaim children from their private paths and differing denominational backgrounds to create a unified identity—a common philosophy "to be shared by Americans of every background and persuasion."[59] Mann was responsible for the country's first compulsory schooling in Massachusetts,[60] which soon spread to other states. His views on using schools to change society were clear when he said: "Men are cast-iron, but children are wax."[61] And the antipathy toward parents upon which these laws were predicated is evident in the words of the editor of a Massachusetts paper encouraging just such a law:

> In too many instances the parents are unfit guardians of their own children. If left to their direction the young will be brought up in idle, dissolute, vagrant habits, which will make them worse members of society than their parents are; instead of filling our public schools, they will find their way into our prisons, houses of correction and almshouses. Nothing can operate effectually here but stringent legislation, thoroughly carried

---

Journal, September 28, 2006, https://www.brusselsjournal.com/node/1389.

59. Lawrence A. Cremin, *The Transformation of the School: Progressivism in American Education, 1876–1957* (New York: Vintage Books, 1961), 10–11.

60. This was the state of Massachusetts, but the colony had previously passed the Old Deluder Satan Act in 1647 in an effort to cultivate biblical literacy. The law, which later spread to other colonies, required towns of a certain size to fund and hire a teacher for the children in the area.

61. Mary Tyler Peabody Mann, *The Life of Horace Mann* (Boston: Walker, Fuller & Company, 1865), 83.

> out by an efficient police; the children must be gathered up and forced into school, and those who resist or impede this plan, whether parents or priests, must be held accountable and punished.[62]

What compulsory schooling did was lay a foundational groundwork for ideological indoctrination to be industrialized—a systematic manipulation of the malleable "wax" Mann spoke of. Education reformers like John Dewey found fertile soil in the early twentieth century to impose their views and create school systems that would lead to their desired social outcomes. Dewey's *Pedagogic Creed* demonstrates the thinking behind his significant influence:

> I believe that every teacher should realize the dignity of his calling; that he is a social servant set apart for the maintenance of proper social order and the securing of the right social growth. I believe that in this way the teacher always is the prophet of the true God and the usherer in of the true kingdom of God.[63]

Dewey, an atheist, was not referring to Christ. In his utopia, the opinions of the masses were the correct barometer for determining what the rising generation should be taught as truth and virtue. His religion was secular humanism—a philosophy that denies the existence of God and emphasizes sensory perception in truth-seeking—and Dewey promoted it by wrapping it in flowery prose. He wanted to persuade Christians to overlook the ultimate goals of the "kingdom" his preferred "prophets" would really be building. Dewey's statement is reflective of his contemporary counterparts, who collectively shaped the early development of the modern public educational system. In 1928 Dewey heaped praise on the Soviets for their "marvelous developments" in promoting "progressive" education.[64] He loved that the schools had a role "in building up forces . . . whose natural effect is to undermine the importance and uniqueness of family life."[65] Dewey and his like-minded pseudo-philosophers saw application for these principles at home in America where, he said, "the increase of importance of public schools has been at least coincident with the relaxation of older family ties."[66] This, to Dewey, was

62. William Swan, *The Massachusetts Teacher, vol. iv* (Boston: Samuel Coolidge, 1851), 291.
63. Jo Ann Boydston, ed., *The Early Works of John Dewey, vol 5* (Carbondale: Southern Illinois University Press, 2008), 95.
64. Joseph Ratner, ed., *Characters and Events: Popular Essays in Social and Political Philosophy* (New York: H. Holt and Co., 1929), 405.
65. Jo Ann Boydston, ed., *The Later Works of John Dewey, vol. 3* (Carbondale: Southern Illinois University Press, 2008), 230.
66. Ibid., 409.

a successful accomplishment. Those who pioneered the modern educational system did not seek to establish intellectual rigor and academic integrity as a foundation. For them, as a prominent official in the National Education Association wrote, "the major function of the school is the social orientation of the individual. It must seek to give him understanding of the transition to a new social order."[67] That "new social order"—complete with its government-anointed "prophets" promoting a counterfeit "kingdom"—is one in which good is denigrated as evil, evil is promoted as good, and God is pushed to the sidelines through the elevation of secular, humanist, socialist principles.

It is little wonder, then, that for Christians, who are required to love God "with all [their] mind,"[68] it is "spiritually unsafe to attend public schools."[69] Caesar wishes to divert God's children from knowing and serving Him, and how better to do so than to be the primary provider of their education? "Train up a child in the way he should go," says the proverb, "and when he is old, he will not depart from it."[70] Of course, a child "trained up" in a Caesarean culture will not likely depart from it, either. But the state's role in education is counterfeit, in that Caesar's true goal is not edification. Instead he seeks to induce submission, and that ultimately requires ignorance, for his goal to obtain power over us is like "a weed that grows only in the vacant lots of an abandoned mind."[71] So while God desires that we "obtain a knowledge of history, and of countries, and of kingdoms, of laws of God and man, and all this for the salvation of Zion,"[72] the aim of Caesar's schools, in the words of one cynic, "is not to spread enlightenment at all—it is simply to reduce as many individuals as possible to the same safe level, to breed a standard citizenry, to put down dissent and originality."[73]

Despite years of schooling for each child, after the schooling system has had many decades of opportunity for refinement and improvement, the product of public schooling is increasingly mediocre, ignorant individuals often incapable of basic knowledge comprehension. So agreed the National Commission on Excellence in Education, which concluded after

---

67. Quoted in Rod Paige, *The War Against Hope: How Teacher Unions Hurt Children, Hinder Teachers, and Endanger Public Education* (Nashville: Thomas Nelson, 2006), 29.
68. Matthew 22:37.
69. Boyd K. Packer, David O. McKay Symposium, Brigham Young University, October 9, 1996.
70. Proverbs 22:6.
71. Ayn Rand, *Atlas Shrugged* (New York: Random House: 1957), 1045.
72. Doctrine and Covenants 93:53; 88:79.
73. H.L. Mencken, "The Little Red Schoolhouse," *The American Mercury, vol. 1* (New York: Alfred Knoff, 1924) 504.

an eighteen-month study that "[the] educational foundations of our society are presently being eroded by a rising tide of mediocrity that threatens our very future as a nation and as a people."[74]

Today's schools are secular seminaries of learning, complete with "robes of a false priesthood"[75] and pedagogical "prophets" as Dewey designed, leading countless children into helping build a "kingdom" of some sort, but not Christ's. God's children are, through compulsory schooling, compelled by Caesar to be indoctrinated not with God's doctrine but a secular substitute. Christians are typically compelled to send their children to these institutions, but many would do so willingly anyway, enticed for various reasons by the perceived benefits offered. And so the rising generation is captured in a system where the culture of Caesar can be daily reinforced—with sins of commission, as in pledges of allegiance and instruction about the supposedly positive feats and features of government, and sins of omission, as in the lack of any exposure for students to the devilish, destructive, and even deadly aspects of Caesar and his institutions.

Christian children are effectively taught a competing and counterfeit religion, where Caesar is god and God's role in the creation of our world, its history, and the affairs of its people, is entirely absent. "He that is not with me," Jesus said, "is against me,"[76] but too few Christians contemplate what this means in the context of their precious children's education. Caesar's counterfeit seminaries—government schools—might then be seen as the "great gates of hell," for "every institution in which men are not unceasingly occupied with the Word of God must become corrupt."[77] For all the well-meaning people working within the system, its nature and purpose is that of a cheap counterfeit.

Marriage

"What therefore God hath joined together," Jesus said, "let not man put asunder."[78] Marriage is central to God's plan, since "it is not good that

74. "A Nation at Risk: The Imperative for Educational Reform," The National Commision on Excellence in Education, April 1983.
75. Hugh Nibley, "Leaders and Managers," Brigham Young University Commencement Speech, August 19, 1983, https://speeches.byu.edu/talks/hugh-nibley/leaders-managers/.
76. Matthew 12:30.
77. Martin Luther, quoted in *History of the Reformation of the Sixteenth Century* (London: Religious Tract Society, 1856), 190.
78. Mark 10:9.

the man should be alone."[79] The union of man and woman is "ordained of God"[80] and the foundation of family life. But Caesar has intervened in the relationship and positioned himself as the one doing the "joining." It is with his supposed authority that ministers and marriage officiants of all kinds tell couples, "By the power vested in me by the state of [state name], I now pronounce you husband and wife." It is the secular state that purports to marry couples—even those exchanging vows in a church or temple, or under the direction of clergy.

Caesar also assumes the authority to tell certain people they cannot marry at all, for the power to license an activity is the power to deny someone the ability to engage in that activity. Just as Caesar prohibits a person from building a home on their property without a permit, or punishes children for operating a lemonade stand without a business license or food handler's permit, he also requires consenting couples to seek his blessing to approve their union. The basis for beginning to require state permission to marry was specifically to enforce prohibitions against white people marrying blacks, "mulattos," Japanese, Chinese, Indians, Mongolians, or Filipinos.[81] Laws in many of the states had long been in place to outright prohibit such mixing of the races. Maryland was the first,[82] enacting prohibitions in 1664. In Virginia, interracial marriage was banned in 1691.[83] By becoming the arbiter of marriage and imposing a licensure requirement, Caesar was able to "prevent illegal and unlawful marriages."[84]

Over time, what had historically been a sacred institution, regulated by families and churches, became a function of the state. Licensure is inherently exclusionary; licenses exist so that they can be denied to some people. The state gives drivers licenses to some people so it can prohibit others from driving on its roads. The state gives licenses to certain food establishments so it can deny others from offering their culinary services. It requires licenses for marriage so that it can deny marriage to certain individuals. And while the early decades of marriage licensure routinely facilitated denial to people

79. Abraham 5:14; Moses 3:18.
80. Doctrine and Covenants 49:15.
81. "Marriage license," Familypedia, accessed June 12, 2020, https://familypedia.wikia.org/wiki/Marriage_license.
82. "Maryland Enacts First Anti-Interracial Marriage Law," LegalFlip.com, accessed June 12, 2020, http://www.legalflip.com/ThisDayInTheLaw.aspx?id=271.
83. "Racial Integrity Laws (1924–1930)," Encyclopedia Virginia, accessed June 12, 2020, https://www.encyclopediavirginia.org/racial_integrity_laws_of_the_1920s.
84. "Marriage, History of," North Carolina History Project, accessed June 12, 2020, https://northcarolinahistory.org/encyclopedia/marriage-history-of/.

of different races, it is not entirely relegated to history; one interracial couple in Louisiana was denied permission to marry as recently as 2009. "I'm not a racist," the license-denying judge said. "I just don't believe in mixing the races that way."[85]

Caesar's claim to dictate which marriages are lawful also has religious implications. Consider the biblical practice of polygamy, which was practiced in modern times by some early Latter-day Saints. The federal government banned plural marriage through the Morrill Anti-Bigamy Act in 1862, targeting a practice widely considered one of the "twin relics of barbarism"[86] on par with slavery. Years later, George Reynolds offered himself as a test case to pursue the matter in the courts. While married to one woman, he additionally married another in the Utah territory. Convicted of the practice in 1875 and sentenced to two years of hard labor in prison, along with a fine of $500, he lost his court battles at every step, including the US Supreme Court, where the black-robed attorneys called "justices" unanimously upheld his conviction. "Can a man excuse his practices to the contrary [of the law] because of his religious belief?" questioned the Court.

> To permit this would be to make the professed doctrines of religious belief superior to the law of the land, and in effect to permit every citizen to become a law unto himself. Government could exist only in name under such circumstances.[87]

Imagine God ordaining a marriage but Satan stepping in to deny the union. This is the functional equivalent of Caesar's counterfeit role in marriage today.

As with many other things, Caesar encumbers his offerings with incentives to entice willing participation and deter dissent. In the case of marriage, those who obtain a government license unlock perks not available to other couples: tax deductions, hospital visitation rights, inheritance, social security and disability benefits, and more. So pervasive is this practice now that only a handful of jurisdictions recognize a "common law" marriage, in which a couple weds without obtaining a license. Churches have seemingly given up the practice of marrying couples under God's authority, instead ensuring they are "legally and lawfully wedded" under the state's

---

85. "Interracial Couple Denied Marriage License," NBC News, October 15, 2009, http://www.nbcnews.com/id/33332436/ns/us_news-life/t/interracial-couple-denied-marriage-license/.

86. Dorus Morton Fox, *History of Political Parties, National Reminiscences, and the Tippecanoe Movement* (Des Moines: Iowa Printing Co., 1895), 194.

87. *Reynolds v. United States*, 98 U.S. 145 (1878).

purview and with its permission. It should also be considered worrisome when churches defer to Caesar in this regard, predicating their marriage ordinances on government licensure. When a church says that "a couple must obtain a legal marriage license"[88] before that church will solemnize the couple's union in front of God, this shows unnecessary deference that renders far more to Caesar than he is due. Must a committed, consenting couple bow down before the state to seek its blessing, or should they instead only kneel upon God's altar to ask for His?

Caesar's decrees change with the shifting political winds, as in the case of the state altering the nature of marriage to include same-sex couples. If Christians bind themselves and defer to Caesar's control of marriage, accepting his counterfeit practice as a prerequisite, then can they really complain when he changes the practice in ways they do not like? What if Caesar compels churches to officiate same-sex unions, to which they object? Those who subordinate themselves to state control may not like the various outcomes that arise. In effect, ceding to this counterfeit allows Caesar to "put asunder" what God has ordained. Christians ought to be wary of letting Caesar have any control when it comes to sacred ordinances God has established and encouraged.

Welfare

"God hath given a commandment that all men should have charity,"[89] a point the scriptures repeatedly reinforce. Those who are not charitable with the resources under their stewardship are of no worth[90] and cannot inherit what God has prepared for them.[91] We are to "give to him that asketh"[92] and "impart of [our] substance to the poor, every man according to that which he hath."[93] God is pleased "that he hath given all these things unto man; for unto this end were they made to be used."[94] The earth "is full" of resources for His children, and "there is enough and to spare; yea, I prepared all things, and have given unto the children of men to be agents unto

88. "General Handbook: Serving in The Church of Jesus Christ of Latter-day Saints" (Salt Lake City: The Church of Jesus Christ of Latter-day Saints, 2020), 216.
89. 2 Nephi 26:30.
90. Alma 34:29.
91. Ether 12:34.
92. Matthew 5:42.
93. Mosiah 4:26.
94. Doctrine and Covenants 59:20.

themselves."[95] With this agency, and as stewards[96] of God's resources, He entrusts us with an obligation to share with those in need.[97] The "world lieth in sin" because people should not "possess that which is above another."[98] "If any man shall take of the abundance which I have made," God continues, "and impart not his portion, according to the law of my gospel, unto the poor and the needy, he shall, with the wicked, lift up his eyes in hell, being in torment."[99] The commandment to help the poor is an individual mandate, not an institutional one. We cannot outsource this obligation, for all men, each of their own accord, "should have charity"[100] to attain salvation.[101] God directs every person to "love thy neighbour as thyself"[102] in order to practice their "pure religion."[103]

Before Caesar's aggressive intervention into the area of welfare, individuals tried their best to fulfill these mandates and serve those in need. In early America, for example, the "three-legged stool of family, church, and neighborhood"[104] helped care for the needy in a pattern that "rested on an ethical principle of reciprocity,"[105] where self-reliance was the goal.[106] Alexis de Tocqueville's observations show the contrast between "free institutions" providing aid, versus the Caesarean approaches throughout Europe where the "state almost exclusively undertakes to supply bread to the hungry, assistance and shelter to the sick, work to the idle, and to act as the sole reliever of all kinds of misery."[107] Whereas governments elsewhere had dominated the provision of welfare, "in the United States, you will be sure to find an association."[108] It was extremely common for those in need to form and join fraternal associations that provided health care, life insurance, and other benefits. More than just "a white male phenomenon,"[109] these organizations

95. Doctrine and Covenants 104:17.
96. Doctrine and Covenants 104:13.
97. Matthew 5:42; Mosiah 4:26; 18:27; Doctrine and Covenants 56:16.
98. Doctrine and Covenants 49:20.
99. Doctrine and Covenants 104:18.
100. 2 Nephi 26:30.
101. Moroni 10:21.
102. Mark 12:31.
103. James 1:27.
104. Marvin Olasky, *The Tragedy of American Compassion* (Washington, D.C.: Regnery Publishing, 1992), 13.
105. David T. Beito, *From Mutual Aid to the Welfare State: Fraternal Societies and Social Services, 1890–1967* (Chapel Hill: University of North Carolina Press, 2003), 3.
106. Ibid, 29.
107. Olasky, *The Tragedy of American Compassion*, 22.
108. Beito, *From Mutual Aid to the Welfare State*, 5.
109. Ibid., 3.

were intensely popular among immigrants, minorities, and the working class. Their prime object was "to promote the brotherhood of man . . . to establish a system for the care of the widows and orphans, the aged and disabled, and enable every worthy member to protect himself from the ills of life."[110] In 1910, their combined membership surpassed 13 million;[111] observers noted that such organizations "honeycombed the slums of Chicago" and among one ethnic minority the "number of societies passes computation," while the Lower East Side of Manhattan "swarms with voluntary organizations of many kinds."[112]

The prevalence of such spontaneously organized societies was often a manifestation of the attempts by their participants to fulfill their Christian religion. One such association dedicated itself, in addition to rendering aid to needy members, to "Christianity, education, morality and temperance and the art of governing, self reliance, and true manhood and womanhood."[113] But it would be a mistake to think that such welfare was predominantly administered by formal organizations.

> Reciprocal relief was far more prevalent than either governmental or private hierarchical relief. Its most basic expression was informal giving, the countless and unrecorded acts of kindness from neighbors, fellow employees, relatives, and friends. The precise magnitude of informal giving can never be known, but it was undeniably vast. A study of 200 wage-earning families in New York City conducted in 1905 revealed that "almost every family of small income received some help or other from friends or relatives in the form of clothing for the children, money for the rent, or occasional gifts to carry the family over a tight place." According to the study, informal giving aided so many that it was fallacious to classify families into distinct categories such as "dependent" or "independent." The assistance provided through church congregations included many elements of reciprocal relief. It often appeared in spontaneous and unrecorded guises. Help came from collection plates and via such monetary intangibles as job information, homes for orphans, barn raising, and temporary housing.[114]

These informal arrangements "dwarfed the efforts of formal social welfare agencies."[115] In effect, they were a passive manifestation of individuals'

---

110. Ibid., 28.
111. Ibid., 14.
112. Ibid., 20.
113. Ibid., 182.
114. Ibid., 19.
115. Ibid.

efforts to discharge this divine obligation. This mutual aid was reciprocal in nature—people helping one another in a Zion-like attempt to achieve equality. It is often believed that equality, in the context of physical possessions, means the redistribution of tangible assets evenly until all are held alike, but the apostle Paul had a much different take on the term:

> For I mean not that other men be eased, and ye burdened: But by an equality, that now at this time your abundance may be a supply for their want, that their abundance also may be a supply for your want: that there may be equality.[116]

In other words, we achieve equality not through making sure that each person has the same amount and type of things as everybody else, but by freely offering resources, talents, and time to others in need. No middlemen need be involved, for the most rewarding and uplifting forms of charity are those that allow giver and receiver to both benefit through their intimate exchange of one's abundance becoming another's supply. God doesn't require that we all have exactly the same amount of things, but that we freely share His gifts with one another, offering our supplies to those in need. This anti-poverty program means that rather than "us" giving "our" supplies to somebody in need, we simply offer God's property to another one of His children in need. We are mere stewards of what God has allowed us to acquire. But the transaction is one of true mutual aid, for the "abundance" Paul refers to is not merely temporal. When a giver provides physical support to a receiver, the receiver often becomes the reciprocal giver—providing spiritual support to the other person, creating a much more significant equality than is suggested by the mere redistribution of physical goods.

Times of crisis are when would-be saviors thrive, offering themselves as the proper problem solvers to an ignorant public desperate for help. So it was when the Great Depression led to a Caesarean intervention unlike any seen before in the area of welfare: the creation of the welfare state that has grown tremendously ever since. Even in the early days of this encroachment by the state, fraternal societies "were in full retreat as social welfare institutions." By assuming the burden of caring for those in need, "governments had undermined much of the reason for the existence of societies and thus for people to join."[117] The role of churches "shrank dramatically with the expansion in government spending under the New Deal," with the data clearly showing that "higher government spending leads to lower church

116. 2 Corinthians 8:13–14.

117. Beito, *From Mutual Aid to the Welfare State*, 231.

charitable activity."[118] In fact, church welfare spending "fell by 30 percent in response to the New Deal."[119] The leaders of these fraternal organizations feared this outcome, where "much was lost in an exchange"[120] after that exchange shifted to Caesar's domain. The old system had "transcended monetary calculations."[121] But since Caesar's intervention, "The old relationships of voluntary reciprocity and autonomy have slowly given way to paternalistic dependency."[122] Those caring for the elderly and orphans cited new welfare programs "as justification not only for rejecting applicants but for closing down entirely."[123]

Charity declines as the obligation is outsourced to the corrupt and inefficient state.[124] Private philanthropy is crowded out by Caesar,[125] for it is extremely difficult, if not economically untenable, to compete against an institution that asserts the power to compel everyone to assist. And so as charity became "as cold as the payment of taxes,"[126] Caesar's counterfeit undermined the ennobling aspects of charity. People felt, and feel, like they are sufficiently supportive of the poor among them because they are taxed for that alleged purpose, and in the process they become "a mere bystander, a mere spectator"[127] to helping the poor. But Caesar is "incapable of approximating the warm handclasp from a fellow member or the friendly visitation of fraternalists to a stricken brother."[128] God doesn't want us to indirectly transfer goods to needy people; He wants us to build relationships and bear one another's burdens.[129] We are to strive for "mutual helpfulness by the building up of an actual sense of brotherhood

---

118. Jonathan Gruber and Daniel M. Hungerman, "Faith-based charity and crowd-out during the great depression," *Journal of Public Economics*, no. 91 (2007), 1.
119. Ibid.
120. Beito, *From Mutual Aid to the Welfare State*, 234.
121. Ibid.
122. Ibid.
123. Ibid., 229.
124. "On average, 70 cents of each dollar budgeted for government assistance goes not to the poor, but to the members of the welfare bureaucracy and others serving the poor." See James Rolph Edwards, "The Costs of Public Income Redistribution and Private Charity," *Journal of Libertarian Studies*, vol. 21, no. 2 (2007), 4.
125. Today there are 126 separate and often overlapping government anti-poverty programs at the federal level alone. See "The American Welfare State: How We Spend Nearly $1 Trillion a Year Fighting Poverty—and Fail," Cato Institute, April 11, 2012, https://www.cato.org/sites/cato.org/files/pubs/pdf/PA694.pdf.
126. Olasky, *The Tragedy of American Compassion*, 150.
127. Ibid, 23.
128. Beito, *From Mutual Aid to the Welfare State*, 230.
129. Galatians 6:2; Mosiah 18:8.

among men,"[130] which is entirely absent when Caesar's counterfeit is the dominant system for rendering aid.

Christians are lulled into charitable inaction by believing that their obligation to help the poor is satisfied through Caesar. Consequently, they miss out on the purpose and benefits of directly helping those in need and prop up a highly inefficient system that has proven itself unable to foster independence and industry among its participants. Like any good counterfeit, it has superficial similarity while lacking the same substance as the original.

Patriotism

Gustave Gilbert was an American psychologist fluent in German. After World War II ended, he was sent to Nuremberg, Germany, as a translator for the International Military Tribunal to assist in the trials of the German World War II prisoners. Hermann Göring, who had been one of the highest-ranking Nazis, was among the prisoners. Göring had been charged with conspiracy, waging a war of aggression, war crimes, and crimes against humanity. Gilbert was appointed to be the prison psychologist, and in that role became a confidant of Göring's, who shared his observations and thoughts, which Gilbert recorded in his diary. During one of their conversations, Göring conceded,

> Naturally, the common people don't want war, but, after all, it is the *leaders* of the country who determine the policy and it is always a simple matter to drag the people along, whether it is a democracy or a fascist dictatorship or a Parliament or a communist dictatorship.[131]

Gilbert protested, pointing out that in America, people have a voice in the process of declaring war through their elected representatives. Göring dismissed this rebuttal outright:

> Oh, that is all well and good, but, voice or no voice, the people can always be brought to the bidding of the leaders. That is easy. All you have to do is tell them they are being attacked, and denounce the pacifists for lack

130. Letter from the First Presidency of The Church of Jesus Christ of Latter Day Saints to the US Treasury Department, October 11, 1941, https://www.connorboyack.com/blog/a-letter-to-the-treasury-from-the-lds-first-presidency-in-1941.
131. G.M. Gilbert, *Nuremberg Diary* (Cambridge: Da Capo Press, Inc., 1995), 278.

> of patriotism and exposing the country to danger. It works the same way in any country.[132]

What is this patriotism of which he spoke? Typically defined as one's "love of country," it is more commonly associated with an expression of loyalty to and support for one's government. Stemming from the Greek *patris*, or fatherland, the word implies a kinship with those who share a geographic or cultural tie. It is generally synonymous with "national pride" and embodies the intertwined sentiments that express affection for one's friends and neighbors, part of a shared culture with a common national identity. But Caesar easily expands patriotism into its close cousin, nationalism—leading people to view their love of country as superior to others; it is a prideful comparison that requires seeing one's kindred as better than others, for whatever reason is most relevant. A patriotic person must sadly "become the enemy of the rest of mankind," for "to wish the greatness of our own country is often to wish evil to our neighbors."[133]

The patriotism so commonly associated with Caesar is thus easily taken advantage of by those in control of the state, as Göring indicated with the superlative "always." No one wants to be considered unpatriotic, of course, for this is tantamount to treason in a Caesarean culture. It suggests ingratitude to the state, because if you do not love your country then you must be chastised for benefiting from Caesar's bounties without reciprocating loyalty and support in return. There are few ways more effective at silencing a person and ensuring their compliance than to accuse them of being insufficiently patriotic when the culture is calling for Caesar's strength and security in response to a perceived threat. Göring knew what he was talking about.

Patriotism thus becomes a counterfeit tool whereby the adversary pits some of God's children against others; brotherly love takes a backseat to pseudo-patriotic tribalism. It is a preference for one's own people at the expense of a higher unity. The home team is always the best, and one ought to support the team with one's actions, words, and feelings. In this counterfeit, "love of country" becomes a wedge between one's own tribe and the rest of humanity. Some go so far as to feel that their culture is exceptional or ideal, to be exported or even imposed upon the unenlightened peoples around the world. The ideals of one's own culture then become something worth fighting and dying for—a psychotic epidemic of sorts that hypnotizes

132. Ibid.

133. Voltaire, *The Works of Voltaire*, vol. 8 (Akron: The Werner Company, 1905), 11.

people into committing barbarities against their own spiritual brothers and sisters. The history of the world reveals that the fruit of patriotism is not peace, but war. "We train a man in the art of war and call him a patriot," falling prey to "Satan's counterfeit of true patriotism, perverting the Savior's teaching"[134] about love. But God commanded us to love Him and one another,[135] not our country.

True patriotism involves loving all of God's children, for the only *patris*, or fatherland, that really matters is our Father's land as a whole, the common identity every person shares with Him. "God is no respecter of persons,"[136] after all. He has made "of one blood all nations of men for to dwell on all the face of the earth."[137] To that end, patriotism is a dangerous counterfeit for the same reason that Satan's temptation to wield power over another is: the Lord said, "Ye shall not esteem one flesh above another, or one man shall not think himself above another."[138] Those who exalt themselves above others "shall be abased,"[139] to guard against the natural man's tendency of "lifting themselves up with their pride, despising others."[140] If we love others as God requires, then our "love of country" cannot be limited to those who submit to the same Caesar, let alone to Caesar himself. And while most Christians would excuse their patriotism by responding that they can love their country while also loving others, Göring's words suggest otherwise.

Our neighborly love shouldn't be defined or confined by arbitrary borders or political affiliations. Thankfully, Christ is the great equalizer and eraser of other identities. All can follow the Way and choose Christ and reject Caesar. Our goal should not be to be a patriotic American or good citizen but rather an earnest seeker of the kingdom of God, following the example of the post-resurrection Nephite society in which there were not "any manner of -ites; but they were in one, the children of Christ, and heirs to the kingdom of God."[141] This is where our focus and fervor should lie—not in the Caesarean conflict that inevitably arises from political tribes and geographical factions that separate God's children. We must rise above this

---

134. Spencer W. Kimball, "The False Gods We Worship," *Ensign*, June 1976.
135. Matthew 22:36–40.
136. Alma 4:12.
137. Acts 17:26.
138. Mosiah 23:7.
139. Doctrine and Covenants 101:42.
140. Mosiah 3:19.
141. 4 Nephi 1:17.

and practice the Golden Rule globally. "Of such patriots, future generations would shout praises, and our Eternal God would pass judgments of glory."[142]

Military

The disciples of the Prince of Peace are paradoxically "a warlike people, easily distracted from our assignment of preparing for the coming of the Lord." As enemies arise, "we commit vast resources to the fabrication of gods of stone and steel—ships, planes, missiles, fortifications—and depend on them for protection and deliverance. When threatened, we become anti-enemy instead of pro-kingdom of God."[143] This is a stinging, though accurate, indictment of a people who have been taught not to trust in the arm of flesh.[144] Indeed, "much of the skill, ingenuity, and ability" of Christians is "devoted to manufacturing instruments of death."[145]

Caesar desires conflict because it provides him an opportunity to offer security to his subjects and remind them of his role in the process. He therefore starts, encourages, and foments war to facilitate this goal. World history is a catalog of one warfare after another; America alone has only been at peace for twenty-one years since it was founded. Put differently, over 90 percent of the country's existence has involved war.[146] And while Caesar holds himself out as protector against foreign foes, it is estimated that in the twentieth century alone, 262 million people were killed by their own government.[147] Most notably, the USSR killed 62 million of its people; China killed 45 million; Nazi Germany killed 21 million; Japan killed 6 million; Cambodia killed 2 million; and the list continues to include many other nations whose repressive regimes physically pitted the state against the individual. Based on the population at the time—over 11 billion people lived during the twentieth century—this means that various Caesars worldwide killed roughly 3.7 percent of the entire human race, or a number equal

142. Russell M. Nelson, "Blessed Are the Peacemakers," *Ensign*, November 2002.
143. Spencer W. Kimball, "The False Gods We Worship;" see also Revelation 9:20.
144. Jeremiah 17:5; Psalm 44:6–8; 2 Nephi 4:34.
145. G. D. Watt and J. V. Long, eds., *Journal of Discourses*, vol. 8 (Liverpool: George Q. Cannon, 1861), 325.
146. "America Has Been at War 93% of the Time—222 out of 239 Years—Since 1776," Global Research, January 20, 2019, https://www.globalresearch.ca/america-has-been-at-war-93-of-the-time-222-out-of-239-years-since-1776/5565946.
147. See R. J. Rummel, *Death by Government* (New Brunswick: Transaction Publishers, 1994).

to over 80 percent of the population of the United States of America at the time. This number of government murders is four times more than the number of people who died in Caesar's wars as active soldiers or as so-called "collateral damage" during all foreign and internal wars during the same century.[148] Caesar's counterfeit of protection is mighty dangerous indeed.

War is inevitable in a fallen world, and though Christians are to abhor it, "peace nearly always has been more a dream than a reality."[149] But God has given a clear commandment on this issue, and those who seek His protection rather than Caesar's counterfeit have instructions to follow. When faced with war, we "should first lift a standard of peace,"[150] bear attacks "patiently and revile not against [the aggressor], neither seek revenge"[151]—a bitter pill to swallow for a culture that condones and encourages retaliatory strikes against one's enemies. Only after three offenses (or acts of aggression) committed against us, each of which we should meet with forgiveness, does the Lord tell us that "thine enemy is in thine hands and thou art justified"[152] in "going out to battle against that nation."[153] Even then, we are encouraged to forgive, sparing our enemy the justice many would say he deserves, with a promise of being "rewarded with righteousness."[154] While this high standard may seem untenable and applicable only to theological states of scriptural history, we are explicitly told that "this is an ensample unto all people, saith the Lord your God, for justification before me."[155] There are no asterisks or exceptions to God's law on the matter; Christians must not strike back.

Fifty-six years after the Declaration of Independence was signed, a community of Latter-day Saint Christians in Missouri was viciously attacked by a mob of their disgruntled neighbors. Having lost their homes, their loved ones, and their possessions, those who survived understandably felt a desire for retaliation and revenge. After all, this latest bout of persecution was not a unique occurrence. Time and again, these people had been subjected to similar oppression. In the midst of

148. See Matthew White, "Historical Atlas of the Twentieth Century," accessed May 12, 2020, http://necrometrics.com/all20c.htm. Roughly 64 million people were killed in or because of combat in international and domestic wars.
149. Joseph B. Wirthlin, "Peace Within," *Ensign*, May 1991, 36.
150. Doctrine and Covenants 98:34.
151. Doctrine and Covenants 98:23.
152. Doctrine and Covenants 98:31.
153. Doctrine and Covenants 98:36.
154. Doctrine and Covenants 98:30.
155. Doctrine and Covenants 98:38.

such intense feelings and contentious circumstances, the Lord gave a revelation in response. Despite the people's strong desire to strike back, God instructed them to "renounce war and proclaim peace."[156] In a world of constant conflict and strong support for military intervention, it is important for Christians to consider how well we renounce the status quo of destruction and death and instead proclaim peace—even when we are threatened or attacked. Do the followers of the Prince of Peace carry His standard in the face of war or do they gladly parade around with the flags and insignia of their respective Caesars?

Christ teaches the Golden Rule, to love even our enemies, while Caesar cultivates and exploits the natural desire[157] for conflict. But Christians "cannot regard war as a righteous means of settling international disputes." We must be "against war," for conflict "should be settled by peaceful means."[158] And yet many still protest, arguing that the individual right of self-defense justifies a broader military response to attacks from foreign enemies, and thus war. But Caesar almost always justifies warfare on such grounds, conjuring up reasons why the enemy is at fault and why he, the victim, must respond in kind. Attacks are fabricated (as in the case of false flag incidents), or provoked, or welcomed by the forces that benefit from conflict—Caesar's military industrial complex. To win popular support, a threat or attack is hyped up using fearmongering and appeals to patriotism. But the scriptures are clear:[159] a Christian cannot believe that "aggression should be carried on in the name and under the false cloak of defense."[160] Caesar is eager to protect people from being stung by hornets, even if he happens to be the one shaking their nest.

Military might is a secular substitute for God's protection, a Caesarean counterfeit leading Christians to believe that they should rely on the arm of flesh. We should not fear our enemies, but rather "fear [our] God and . . . supplicate him for protection."[161] When the King of Assyria attacked Judah, their invading army was much bigger than that of the Jews. But

---

156. Doctrine and Covenants 98:16.
157. Mosiah 3:19.
158. "A Letter to the Treasury from the LDS First Presidency in 1941," Connor's Conundrums, accessed June 13, 2020, https://www.connorboyack.com/blog/a-letter-to-the-treasury-from-the-lds-first-presidency-in-1941.
159. "Preventive War and the Book of Mormon," Connor's Conundrums, accessed June 13, 2020, https://www.connorboyack.com/blog/preventive-war-and-the-book-of-mormon.
160. "A Letter to the Treasury . . ."
161. 3 Nephi 4:10.

King Hezekiah noted that "with him is an arm of flesh, but with us is the Lord our God to help us, and to fight our battles."[162] David echoed similar words when going against Goliath.[163] When the Syrians surrounded Israel with their large host, Elisha's servant was predictably worried. "Alas, my master! how shall we do?" he fretted. Elisha responded: "Fear not: for they that be with us are more than they that be with them."[164] One scriptural story after another reminds us of God's protection for righteous people who seek His strength over Caesar's, who rely on His arm instead of the arm of flesh.

The military presents to Christians perhaps the most seductive of all idols and the most convincing of counterfeits. The "gods of stone and steel" receive our adoration and support, and we view ourselves as dependent on them, while God is rendered comparatively powerless. We worship God as a distant being who helps us when we lose our car keys or when a loved one has cancer, but who is mainly a custodian, keeping heavenly mansions prepared for our arrival. Christians thus relegate the Savior to the spiritual realm only, viewing Him as unable to protect them in the way Caesar clearly can. The counterfeit thus becomes the accepted norm, leading God's people to justify their support of the state in many other ways based on this fundamental role of protecting them from their enemies. Christ is relegated to the back seat in terms of the average believer's consideration of their physical safety, if He is even invited into the vehicle at all.

Followers of the Prince of Peace must recognize that the peace they desire "is not just the absence of war. It is the *opposite* of war."[165] Instead of revering military might and state power, we must see these as Caesar's instruments—counterfeits of God's power to protect and violations of His law for when combat is justified. Contrary to the claims of Caesar's supporters, peacemaking is not the by-product of soldiers, drones, and munitions. It instead comes from living the gospel of Jesus Christ. It requires loving our enemies,[166] forgiving those who have wronged us,[167] raising a standard of peace to those who actually attack us,[168] and in all things renouncing war

162. 2 Chronicles 32:8.
163. 1 Samuel 17:45.
164. 2 Kings 6:14–17.
165. Dallin H. Oaks, "World Peace," *Ensign*, May 1990, 71.
166. Matthew 5:44.
167. Matthew 18:21; Doctrine and Covenants 98:40.
168. Doctrine and Covenants 98:34.

and proclaiming peace.[169] Peace is contrary to the culture of Caesar and inherent to Christian worship.

Standing armies and military aggression are therefore a systematized rejection of Christ's commandment to love one another. Those who "take the sword shall perish with the sword,"[170] He taught. Caesar counterfeits this counsel, providing ample justifications and flattering arguments as to why a military response, even preventatively, is appropriate and deserved. Throughout the Old Testament we see many examples of sword-based politics failing to be a viable method for sustaining God's people and exemplifying and evangelizing His teachings. Christ came to counteract this trend and point out how Caesar's method is the counterfeit. We ought to listen.

169. Doctrine and Covenants 98:16.
170. Matthew 26:52.

CONCLUSION

God's servants have long tried to persuade His children to aspire to and live a higher standard, but many people "will fly to pieces like glass as soon as anything comes that is contrary to their traditions."[1] Throughout the scriptures, prophets have expressed frustration at the unwillingness of people to abandon the "traditions of their fathers" and a counterfeit culture that leads away from God. Nephi was unable to continue teaching and was instead "left to mourn because of the unbelief, and the wickedness, and the ignorance, and the stiffneckedness of men; for they will not search knowledge, nor understand great knowledge, when it is given unto them in plainness, even as plain as word can be."[2] The brother of Jared was required to hide knowledge from others, which was "forbidden to come unto the children of men."[3] Moroni lamented those who had "rejected the gospel of Christ," leading to a commandment from God that he deny them access to past revelations.[4] Mormon wanted to teach "greater things" but "the Lord forbade it, saying: I will try the faith of my people."[5] The Jaredite people "hardened their hearts, and would not hearken" to God's commandments, so "the prophets mourned and withdrew from among the people."[6] Nephites mourned their Lamanite neighbors "because of their

1. Joseph Smith, as quoted in *History of The Church of Jesus Christ of Latter-day Saints*, vol. 6 (Salt Lake City: Deseret News, 1912), 185.
2. 2 Nephi 32:7.
3. Ether 4:1; 3:21.
4. Ether 4:3.
5. 3 Nephi 26:6–11.
6. Ether 11:13.

iniquities and their traditions,"[7] which "caused them to remain in their state of ignorance"[8] and thus not believe in Christ. Alma noted that prophets were "laid under a strict command that they shall not impart [the mysteries of God] . . . unto the children of men" except "according to the heed and diligence which they give unto him,"[9] and yet the people repeatedly proved themselves less than diligent. Jesus even told his disciples, "I have yet many things to say unto you, but ye cannot bear them now."[10]

For all the mystery-revealing and truth-sharing prophets can do for a worthy people, one of their most important roles, especially in situations involving a less-than-worthy people, is "to remind the people that they are in exile," a fact we are apparently prone to forget. "It is easy to become so comfortable in Babylon that we forget our true home"[11]—content to live in our Babylonian summer cottages,[12] while thinking that we are not actually taking up residence on the wrong side of the border. But God calls His people to flee from Babylon and the "nations [that] have drunken of her wine."[13] Indeed, as "all the nations"[14] follow the Caesarean cult and normalize behavior that is inconsistent with God's law, Christianity also becomes contaminated—commingled with Caesar's counterfeits and justified by God's followers, who excuse countless small deviations until they embrace a set of beliefs and actions that is far off course from the Christian standard.

Is this standard too utopian? Is it like Christ's commandment to "be ye therefore perfect"[15]—a goal that is actually unattainable in this life? Should we therefore accommodate and justify a lifestyle that embraces Caesar in certain circumstances, while committing to Christ in the rest? John's revelation calling us to flee Babylon also reminds us of Christ's disapproval of those who are "neither cold nor hot"[16]—those who teeter between two masters, trying to placate both without choosing one or the other. Rejecting Caesar and his satanic support system is therefore the imperative; being

---

7. Alma 19:14.
8. Alma 9:16.
9. Alma 12:9.
10. John 16:12; see also Doctrine and Covenants 19:22.
11. Craig M. Watts, *Bowing Toward Babylon: The Nationalistic Subversion of Christian Worship in America* (Eugene: Cascade Books, 2017), x.
12. Maxwell, *A Wonderful Flood of Light.*
13. Revelation 18:3–4; 3 Nephi 20:41; 2 Corinthians 6:17.
14. 1 Samuel 8:20.
15. Matthew 5:48; see also Jeffrey R. Holland, "Be Ye Therefore Perfect—Eventually," *Ensign*, November 2017.
16. Revelation 3:15–16.

perfectly consistent in our rejection is not. Just as faith and repentance and hope and charity are all daily choices and actions we must incorporate into our life, so too is our choice of Christ over Caesar.

It is likely impossible to fully avoid Caesar or steer clear of his influences and assertions of authority over us, for they are pervasive and persistent. And it is a prudent strategy to comply with Caesar to varying degrees. Christ counseled those following him to "make to yourselves friends of the mammon of unrighteousness,"[17] so that "they will not destroy you."[18] This instruction, in part, enables Christians to "have power and influence with the unrighteous,"[19] so that some of those seduced by Caesar can be persuaded to repent and choose Christ. Total noncompliance with the state would no doubt incur the state's wrath, leading to one of two outcomes. The first is cultural irrelevance, or being considered a fringe part of society that others want no part of. This fringe status reduces our "power and influence." And the second outcome is an outright attack against us and potential extermination. We know God's followers are commanded to "waste and wear out our lives in bringing to light all the hidden things of darkness,"[20] which could easily entail a near-constant condemnation of Caesar, but "it is not always wise to relate all the truth," due to the punitive consequences we would inevitably incur.

> Even Jesus, the Son of God, had to refrain from doing so, and had to restrain His feelings many times for the safety of Himself and His followers, and had to conceal the righteous purposes of His heart in relation to many things pertaining to His Father's kingdom.[21]

But an outward deference to Caesar to ensure our safety—so we can carry on with our work of serving others and spreading the gospel—does not require and should not involve us sharing our hearts or feeling loyal or supportive of Caesar in any way. You "can make to yourselves friends of the mammon of unrighteousness without being unrighteous yourself."[22] Like a person held hostage by an assailant, it is wise to follow Caesar's orders to survive, but it may be advantageous to seek

17. Luke 16:9.
18. Doctrine and Covenants 82:22.
19. Joseph F. Smith, *Journal of Discourses*, vol. 24 (Liverpool: John Henry Smith, 1884), 248.
20. Doctrine and Covenants 123:13.
21. Smith, *History*, 608.
22. Mathias Cowley, in *Seventy-first Semi-Annual Conference of The Church of Jesus Christ of Latter-day Saints* (Salt Lake City: Deseret News, 1900), 23.

opportunities to resist and frustrate his plans. Open insurrection against the state is unwise, but a sincere Christian should not support or participate in Caesar's conquests and spoils.

While Christ frees us[23] from the forces that seek our bondage,[24] Satan tempts us "to seek for power, and authority, and riches, and the vain things of the world."[25] Consequently, through Caesar, people become "oppressed, every one by another, and every one by his neighbor."[26] This is not to say this oppression is the result of evil people aggressively seeking to control others. In truth, Caesar's supporters are by and large sincere, well-meaning people trying to address social ills that plague humanity. Their mistake is in relying on a Caesarean, coercive approach to addressing problems rather than seeking Christ-centered solutions rooted in persuasion and love. They idolize the "works of their hands"[27]—government bureaucracies, policy proposals, civic institutions, and more—rather than doing things God's way. In short, they lack faith in Christ. The existence of Caesar's state, and the broad support it has, is a manifestation of humanity's lack of trust in God. Just as trusting God is an act of faith, so too is trusting Caesar an act of faith of its own kind—faith not in love and forgiveness, but in coercion and control. The Christian course is clear: our faith "should not stand in the wisdom of men, but in the power of God."[28]

Of course, "faith, if it hath not works, is dead."[29] Christians cannot simply give lip service to believing in Christ. They must "bring forth fruit and works meet for [God's] kingdom."[30] Our actions must be consistent with our claims of loving and serving God and our neighbors, for if Christians continue to support Caesar, participate in his processes, use his power over others, and share in his spoils, then they "profess that they know God; but in works they deny him."[31] They "draw near [God] with their mouth, and with their lips do honor [Him], but have removed their heart far from [Him]."[32] Jesus had few nice things to say about hypocrites who "reject the commandment of God, that [they] may keep [their] own tradition,"[33]

23. Galatians 5:1; Mosiah 5:8; Doctrine and Covenants 88:86; 98:8.
24. 2 Nephi 1:13; 2:29; 28:22; Alma 41:11.
25. 3 Nephi 6:15.
26. Isaiah 3:5.
27. Revelation 9:20.
28. 1 Corinthians 2:5.
29. James 2:17.
30. Doctrine and Covenants 101:100; Matthew 3:8.
31. Titus 1:16.
32. Isaiah 29:13;
33. Mark 7:9.

and the Caesarean cult certainly qualifies as a long-standing tradition that implies a rejection of God's commandments. It is a foundational tradition that Satan relies on to amass power over others. It is an institutionalized oppression "supported and urged on and upheld by the influence of that spirit which hath so strongly riveted the creeds of the fathers, who have inherited lies, upon the hearts of the children, and filled the world with confusion."[34] This systemic force that deceives so many "has been growing stronger and stronger, and is now the very mainspring of all corruption, and the whole earth groans under the weight of its iniquity."[35]

The adversary certainly wants us to follow "after the tradition of men, after the rudiments of the world, and not after Christ."[36] But the culturally reinforced and broadly accepted traditions that steer society away from God are actually self-imposed "handcuffs, and chains, and shackles, and fetters of hell."[37] Though the enemy is eager to enslave us, it is our own choice that commits us either to Christ or to Caesar. We are perpetually presented with a duality of persuasion or control, love or hate, truth or counterfeit, "good or evil, life or death."[38] We are "free to choose liberty and eternal life, through the great Mediator of all men, or to choose captivity and death, according to the captivity and power of the devil."[39] But choosing who we will serve[40] is complicated, for life is more comfortable in the middle, halting "between two opinions"[41] without fully committing to either. This attempt at Caesarean compromise is a choice in and of itself, for in God's words, "they who are not for me are against me."[42]

We cannot serve two masters[43]—it is time to choose whose side we are on.

34. Doctrine and Covenants 123:7.
35. Ibid.
36. Colossians 2:8.
37. Doctrine and Covenants 123:8.
38. Alma 29:5.
39. 2 Nephi 2:27.
40. Joshua 24:15.
41. 1 Kings 18:21.
42. 2 Nephi 10:16.
43. Matthew 6:24.

EPILOGUE

While many who share my faith seem to shy away from using the cross in artwork or other visual depictions—wanting to focus on Christ's resurrection rather than His death—I selected the image for the cover of this book with a specific purpose in mind.

The Roman Empire was notorious for using crucifixion as a method of capital punishment, typically reserved for slaves and enemies of the state. Victims were stripped of their clothing, scourged, forced to carry part or all of the cross that they were then nailed to and suspended from. The process sometimes took days, furthering the humiliation that was intended by this painful spectacle. This method of execution was the state's *summum supplicium*, or ultimate punishment, ranked by the Jewish historian Josephus as "the most pitiable of deaths,"[1] worse than being burned alive or beheaded.

Rather than repudiate this symbol of the state, Jesus recalibrated and appropriated it. Despite its association with death, the cross "transformed into a symbol capable of expressing a variety of life-giving meanings for Christians."[2] Jesus taught that any disciple seeking to follow Him should "take up his cross and follow me."[3] But what does it mean to take up one's cross? He explained that a person must "deny himself all ungodliness, and every worldly lust, and keep my commandments."[4] We must "forsake the world [to] save [our] souls,"[5] choosing Christ over all other counterfeits and

1. Josephus, *The Jewish War* (Oxford: Oxford University Press, 2017), 356
2. Donald Senior, *Why the Cross?* (Abingdon Press, 2014), 11.
3. Matthew 16:24; 3 Nephi 12:30.
4. Joseph Smith Translation, Matthew 16:26.
5. Joseph Smith Translation, Matthew 16:29.

competing gods. Taking up our cross means "daily denying ourselves the appetites of the flesh"—not just sexual lust and the temptations of material wealth, but also the natural desire to wield power over others.

The cross can therefore represent both Caesar and Christ. It represents the satanic state—with its aggression and lust for power over others—while also serving as a metaphor for overcoming these worldly forces that distract us from our path toward returning to God. Jesus did not shy away from the metaphorical usefulness of the cross, therefore neither should we. It serves as a reminder that the adversary's claim to power is counterfeit and that, with God, we can "overcome all things [to] be lifted up at the last day."[6]

6. Doctrine and Covenants 75:16, 22.

ABOUT THE AUTHOR

Connor Boyack is founder and president of Libertas Institute, a free market think tank in Utah.

Named one of Utah's most politically influential people by *The Salt Lake Tribune*, Connor's leadership has led to dozens of legislative victories spanning a wide range of areas such as privacy, government transparency, property rights, drug policy, education, personal freedom, and more.

A public speaker and author of more than two dozen books, Connor is best known for the widely acclaimed *Tuttle Twins* books, a children's series introducing young readers to economic, political, and civic principles.

Connor lives near Salt Lake City, Utah, with his wife and two homeschooled children.